Modern Muslims

MODERN MUSLIMS

a sudan memoir

Steve Howard

ohio university press • athens

Ohio University Press, Athens, Ohio 45701
ohioswallow.com
© 2016 by Ohio University Press
All rights reserved

To obtain permission to quote, reprint, or otherwise reproduce or
distribute material from Ohio University Press publications,
please contact our rights and permissions department at
(740) 593-1154 or (740) 593-4536 (fax).

Printed in the United States of America
Ohio University Press books are printed on acid-free paper ⊚ ™

26 25 24 23 22 21 20 19 18 17 16   5 4 3 2 1

Library of Congress Cataloging-in-Publication Data
Names: Howard, W. Stephen, author.
Title: Modern Muslims : a Sudan memoir / Steve Howard.
Description: Athens : Ohio University Press, 2016. | Includes
  bibliographical references.
Identifiers: LCCN 2016024897| ISBN 9780821422304 (hc : alk. paper) |
  ISBN 9780821422311 (pb : alk. paper) | ISBN 9780821445778 (pdf)
Subjects: LCSH: Howard, W. Stephen—Religion. | Howard, W.
  Stephen—Travel—Sudan. | Ikhwān al-Jumhūrīyūn. | Sufism—Sudan—
  History—20th century. | Islam—Sudan—History—20th century. |
  Sudan—Politics and government—1956–1985. | Sudan—Social life
  and customs—20th century.
Classification: LCC BP188.8.S8 H69 2016 | DDC 297.409624—dc23
LC record available at https://lccn.loc.gov/2016024897

Contents

Illustrations

Acknowledgments

A book that has emerged slowly over twenty years has accumulated many, many people worthy of my deepest thanks. The enduring hospitality and patience of the brothers and sisters of the Republican Brotherhood movement was of course paramount in making possible the completion of this memoir. I'll single out Abdullahi An-Na'im, Khalid Mohamed El Hassan, and Mustafa El Jaili for their particular assistance in my getting the facts straight—although any misperception is my own. Many other brothers and sisters were eager to help me understand by sharing their understanding, and they are mentioned in the book as well. The Republican brothers and sisters have been the most important teachers in my life.

I also have relied (heavily!) on patient friends in the United States who have listened to me (and listened to me and listened to me) talk about what I was trying to represent with this book. The advice over the many years from Lidwien Kapteijns, Ghirmai Negash, Elizabeth Collins, and Jay Spaulding has been critical in the production of this memoir. My many students who have listened to me talk about this movement and have added their impressions of it—often providing other African examples—have provided a great learning experience for me as well. I am deeply in debt to the marvelous Gill Berchowitz for her tireless championing of Africanist scholarship and my work on this book, as she patiently steered it toward publication. I am also very grateful to Professor Francis Nyamnjoh at the University of Cape Town for providing me time and an office, with a view of Table Mountain, so that I could finally pull this book together.

I dedicate this book to my own siblings, Kathy, Rosemary, and Peter, in hopes that they gain a greater understanding of what their older brother has been up to for a long time.

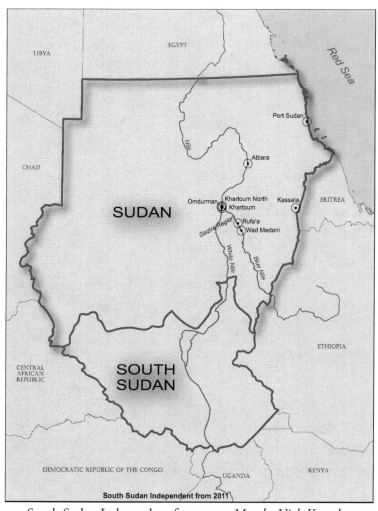

South Sudan Independent from 2011. *Map by Nick Kroncke.*

Prologue

Noon

Of the 114 chapters of the Qur'an, 29 of them begin with stand-alone letters of the alphabet, signifying what humankind is not yet sure. The Arabic letter *noon* (ن) appears in Islam's holy book by itself at the beginning of one of its chapters, challenging the world to uncover knowledge of God that may be just beyond human reach. The letter *noon* also represents the crescent moon in Sufi symbolism, its incompleteness a reminder of the striving in which humans must engage in order to seek but never achieve the complete state of perfection. Perfection is the ultimate goal of this striving, which, not coincidently, may also unlock all of the knowledge contained in the Qur'an. As I encountered the men and women of the Republican Brotherhood in Sudan, I came to think of myself as "*noon*"—very much an incomplete man and unsure of what I was looking for, and eager to be guided. I was also a bit awed by what I perceived to be the brothers' and sisters' already achieved "perfection," or at least by their positive attitudes in the midst of Sudan's deteriorating conditions.

The Qur'an's two shades of meaning, one *zahir,* or revealed, and one hidden, or *batin,* were also intended as a challenge from

God to promote study, prayer, and reflection that would ultimately lead to the understanding of God. I have spent more than thirty years admiring the members of the Republican Brotherhood, who dedicated their lives to improving themselves and the world by uncovering as much of the hidden meaning as God would allow. For a variety of reasons—some clearly spiritual—my sharing in those discoveries was always many steps behind my Sudanese friends.

After living with the brothers from early 1982, my first departure from the group took place at a farewell *jelsa*, or "meeting," in November 1984, in Omdurman at a most difficult time for the members of the Republican Brotherhood. More than fifty Republicans and the movement leader, Mahmoud Mohamed Taha, had been in prison for more than a year because Sudan's President Jaafar Nimeiry anticipated that they would oppose the imposition of his version of Islamic law, put in place in September 1983. In the midst of their political difficulties, the brothers tried to put the best face on my decision to leave for the United States in order to complete work on my PhD degree. Sudan's reputation for warm hospitality had been fully realized in my years in the community; I had grown particularly fond of one of their terms of greeting, *mushtageen* ("you've been missed"), which was used even by people who had seen each other only a day or two before. It could also be used ironically—in the Sudanese sense of humor—accompanied by a sly smile. It had not taken a great deal of negotiation for me to move in with members of the Republican Brotherhood; recruitment was important to the movement, and my joining them was a point of pride. My own inclination was to de-emphasize their pride in me, but I also learned to accept the Sufi code of "let what is done for you be done for you."

The brothers in the house where I lived had invited my favorite *munshid*, or performer of the modern hymns or odes for which the Republicans were well known, to sing in his rich baritone for the evening's farewell. Beds were brought from inside the house to the courtyard for us to sit on. The Republican brothers took departures from the group very seriously. As one left a group of Republicans, the group would raise their arms in farewell while chanting the name of God until the traveler disappeared from view. The group's intense solidarity was the sum of its members' collective focus on the teachings of Mahmoud Mohamed Taha. The departure ritual, which I was to experience countless times over the years, was designed to be a memory, an image to hold in your heart to sustain you until you returned to this group of brothers and sisters or were welcomed by the next one on your journey.

Over the course of three decades of arrivals and departures to and from groups of Republican brothers and sisters, I have tried to make academic sense of what I had seen living with the Republican Brotherhood in Sudan. I wrote many conference papers on the reformist methodology of Mahmoud Mohamed Taha and about this group of men and women and their families who saw themselves as the vanguard in promoting a new approach to Islam's role in the modern world. I sought grants and leave from my teaching to support my writing about the Republicans, and was successful in these requests from time to time. I accepted a Fulbright Senior Scholar award to teach sociology at Bayero University Kano, Nigeria, intending to produce a scholarly book on the Republican movement—in a location far from the distractions of home. I enjoyed the intense Islamic atmosphere in Kano—surprised to find it more conservative than Sudan—but the five chapters I managed to write despite the heat and electricity failures did not satisfy me. My writing struck me as strained and distant.

I think that the many moving parts of this Sudanese movement: its role in Sudan's history, its radical nonviolent challenge to conventional Islam, its many intriguing characters who were my close friends, all weighed heavily on me, making daunting the prospect of my bringing it all together as a compelling book. Sudan's descent into pariah-state status—ethnic cleansing in Darfur, the endless and bloody war in the South, the indefatigably intolerant Islamist government—made me question my desire to be associated with Sudan. It is also worth considering that my slow start in telling this story may have been a function of my discomfort in having an earlier, more religiously observant version of myself confront the dry-eyed current version.

I became determined to get the story of the Republican Brotherhood out as the world became more and more concerned about the rising Muslim voices raised in political rhetoric in the years following Iran's 1979 revolution. I should note that many Republican brothers themselves and other friends were frustrated by my taking so long to tell their story. The Republican narrative was not without its tensions, but it became increasingly difficult for me to see where a small social movement of men and women committed to progressive changes in their society and the peaceful proselytization of their message across a relatively obscure African country, fit into the grand narrative of the "Islamic Threat," particularly after 9/11. Academics, pundits, reporters, preachers, and former presidents had all streamed to the Muslim world to understand, among other things, "Why do they hate us?" Shelves of bookshops in the United States were crowded with such titles by "disgruntled Muslims" as *Infidel,* by Ayaan Hirsi Ali; *A God Who Hates,* by Wafa Sultan; and *The Trouble with Islam,* by Irshad Manji.

As I came to know the men and women of the Republican Brotherhood, I just wanted to understand how to get as close to this progressive movement as possible because it spoke to me intelligently and forcefully as a vital commitment to positive change in Africa. And I was deeply moved by and drawn to the strong sense of community that appeared to be the foundation for the enthusiasm they had for their work. I liked the balance of spiritual conviction and warm Republican social solidarity—which often centered on food—represented in the popular Sudanese saying they often quoted, *mafi din bidun angeen* ("No religion without batter," that is, you can't pray on an empty stomach—it rhymes in Arabic).

Today's determined Western interest in the details of life within Islamic social organizations largely focuses on finance and leadership, a concern for how those two factors ignite the potential for violence, rather than on how members of such groups actually lead their lives or what identifies them as "Islamic." The Republican Brothers and Sisters constructed a comprehensive social system that both allowed them to hone their practice of the teachings of Mahmoud Mohamed Taha and to turn inward in a limited fashion from a society that viewed those practices with some degree of suspicion or incomprehension. The Republican way of life during the era of Mahmoud Mohamed Taha's leadership was an application of his intense search for the meaning of the Qur'an—revealed to the Prophet Mohamed in the seventh century—in today's world. I focus on the mundane details of their lives here in order to give a sense of the everyday, plodding quality of the work of reforming Islam. This work has never proceeded in a linear fashion in Sudan, but rather in halting steps. In the Republican case, those steps were directed out of spaces of their familiar headquarters for thinking, discussing, and engaging in spiritual life and making a contribution to the understanding of and practice of human rights in their country.

The intention of this memoir is to shed light on social change promoted through the vehicle of a modern Islamic movement dedicated to its members' understanding of the pursuit of peace. That social change can be a product of tension between religious orthodoxies and "new understandings" of faith is my central interest while experiencing the impact each has on the other. The Sudanese roots of this movement were deep, so although describing its membership as representative of Sudan would be misleading, the brothers and sisters were leading Muslim lives

5

Noon

guided by a theology of indigenous provenance. The members of the Republican Brotherhood were determined—in the face of Islamic extremism of which they themselves were victims—to provide an example of what they believed an Islamic community should and could be. They joined this movement and built its identity out of a hopeful view of the future, not out of rage, discontent, or grievances against the ruling regime. They had no political agenda except that democracy and human rights were central to their movement's message and practice in every forum that they organized. The Republican view was always that societal-level human rights or democracy could be sustained only when their source was one's personal practice.

My memoir is in part motivated by the fact that the Republican Brotherhood and the work of Mahmoud Mohamed Taha have been largely relegated to footnotes in contemporary studies of Sudan and Islam and/or to unflattering portrayals in a few books and the media. For me, the Republican Brotherhood represents an indigenous expansion of the Islamic intellectual project that drew strength from both opposing colonialism and from the initial colonial investment in education for Sudan's "modernity." Mahmoud Mohamed Taha's fresh understanding of the texts of Islam revealed possibilities for the Sudanese nation. The postcolonial expansion of primary, secondary, and higher education made Taha's progressive message attractive and accessible to people at a variety of social levels.

My title for this memoir, *Modern Muslims,* might raise eyebrows across the Muslim world at the suggestion that I may be perceiving many Muslims as outside of this rubric. In fact, my title reflects the growth of my observation over years of interacting with the Republican Brothers and Sisters, of the intense link between the theology and movement of Mahmoud Mohamed Taha and their role in the struggle to secure a place for Sudan in a postcolonial and just world. The modern state of the Republic of Sudan is in the very name the Republicans gave to their movement. The movement's emphasis on women's rights, human justice, an educated populace, and democratic governance constituted an impressive twentieth-century agenda for an organization dedicated to Islam. But my primary intention with the selection of the term "modern" for the title was to emphasize the dedication that Taha and his followers had to the idea that Islam had always been modern and contemporary. They saw their task as helping society catch up with that fact.

The members of the Republican Brotherhood never contested elections or attained any political office; their only tools were moral suasion based on their understanding of the word of God and their intense effort to serve as a model community dedicated to peace and human equality. They developed a philosophy of living and applied it to marriage and family, birth and death, and every human possibility in between. They invited all to see how they lived their lives or to listen to and read about their philosophy, their *fikr* (ideology) in books, lectures, hymns, and newspapers. They were harassed and imprisoned for their principled stands for political liberty and freedom of conscience. And they organized themselves to divide the labor of the movement and develop special skills to run it, valuing everyone who wanted to participate, while reaching out and speaking to women and young people particularly with their message. The Republicans tried to treat each other, as Khalid El Haj, who was an important movement leader, reminded me, with *a-sadiq, al-muhubba, wa al-ikhlas* (truth, love, and charity). These values were always very much in evidence in the solidarity that characterized the movement; these were people who eschewed ties to their own families in some cases, in favor of spending all of their time with fellow Republicans. And they found reflections of their teacher, Mahmoud Mohamed Taha, in those that they loved.

After many years of reflective frustration, I finally decided to compose a personal account of my experience living with the

Republican Brotherhood, trying to avoid putting the movement in an academic box, while telling their story as a respectful, engaged observing participant. I want to describe how I learned to live as a member of this group of Brothers and Sisters, and what I learned about life in doing so. I feel that this book is my responsibility to those who shared their lives with me, perhaps a testament to the care in their instruction. My philosophy as an academic researcher has always been that "we are part of what we seek to understand," and this memoir is my most forthright expression of that. I witnessed Republican weddings and all-night and pre-dawn meetings, tried to learn their hymns, ate too much of their food, slept in their houses and in the courtyards outside their houses, visited them in prison, greeted their newborns, listened to their stories, and attended their burials. I have been a privileged witness to the dramatic era of change in which they have lived, and it is time to offer an account. Much of my narrative here is in effect an oral history passed down to me from brothers and sisters who took time to tell me what they knew of Ustadh Mahmoud and/or relate their own personal interactions with him and with each other. Although I sometimes heard a variety of versions of the events I describe here, I have tried to present a consensus view. And this interpretation is my own, of course.

In the chapters that follow I provide a perspective on the history of this movement and details of its members' efforts to organize family and movement life against the backdrop of a Sudan at the beginning of the era it is still mired in today, of intolerant rule by an Islamist state. The execution of Mahmoud Mohamed Taha by the Nimeiry regime on January 18, 1985—for trumped-up charges of "apostasy"—signaled in many respects the beginning of the Islamist era that envelops Sudan today. I will describe here the events leading up to that *sharia*-defying act and its impact on Taha's followers. An injunction from the Qur'an—that there should be "no compulsion in religion"—was taken by the Republican Brotherhood as one of its mottos or inspiring principles. And this Qur'anic verse was violated by the government of Sudan and the Islamist organizations that supported it in the act of executing Mahmoud Mohamed Taha. That fundamental conflict is at the heart of this book.

1

Unity

Mahmoud Mohamed Taha (1909–1985) was the founder, leader, and guide of the Republican Brotherhood movement. He is at the center of any description of the Republican Brotherhood, and he plays an important role in this one as well. But for me, as I tell my story from the rear guard of the movement, Taha is high on a pedestal, and I understood him best through the voices of the brothers and sisters in Sudan and in exile who invested their lives in trying to follow his guidance. They taught me about his training as an engineer in the 1930s and his membership in the Graduates Congress, the intellectual movement that led Sudan's independence struggle. He started his own political party to participate in that effort, called the Republican Party, which he then transformed into an Islamic social reform movement in the early 1950s. He wrote and spoke in public about his vision for a modern and peaceful Muslim world, and attracted followers from all over Sudan who became his representatives in disseminating the message of the movement.

As I came to know the Republican movement I was quickly disabused of the idea that I, as a foreigner from the West, might have any privileges of position or representation. I internalized this message a few weeks into my joining the group while returning to Khartoum as a member of my first *wafd*, or "delegation," to the northern city of Atbara. The Republicans took these missions all over Sudan to spread their message of the possibilities of a new direction in Islam and distribute their books on the subject. Our group of about eight brothers had spent ten days in Atbara, a city on the Nile about six hours north of Khartoum by slow-moving train. The Sudanese knew Atbara as the "city of fire and steel" in that it had been a railway terminus and an industrial center of sorts, dedicated to small-scale manufacturing. It remained a working-class city at the junction of the Nile and Atbara Rivers. Our return journey had been tough, riding while perched on our suitcases in a crowded third-class car, eating the dust that blew in from the open windows as the train crossed the August desert. When we reached the station in Khartoum North I anticipated the usual rush of Sudanese hospitality, a shower and a well-deserved hot meal to follow our arduous progress from Atbara. But to my surprise we were taken from the train station immediately to the home of Mahmoud Mohamed Taha in our sorry sweaty, dusty state. I tried unobtrusively to shake the dust that was caked in my hair as we sat in Ustadh Mahmoud's *saloon,* the main room of the house, waiting to report on our trip. I wondered as I listened to the speakers if a grimy appearance was a required part of the Sufi ritual of this reporting session.

My next surprise was my position in the Atbara trip report lineup. Again, I thought that, as a guest, I would have been given an opportunity to speak early in the program. Of course, the leaders of the delegation spoke first, describing how many lectures were given in Atbara, how the crowd received us, how many Republican tracts were sold there, and importantly, how the brothers treated each other during the trip. But then Ustadh Mahmoud continued to call on members of the Atbara delegation to speak to the brothers and sisters assembled in his house to listen to us and our impressions. Again a surprise as some of those called upon were actually younger than I was, a graduate student from the United States! Finally, I figured it out. Brothers were called to speak in the order of their seniority in the movement, an order that was created by Ustadh Mahmoud's sense of the individual's capacity to understand, live, and model the Republican ideology, the path of the Prophet Mohamed. As for me, I was a weeks-old newcomer, *mustajid,* and was not ready to take an early place in the reporting line. But also I realized then that I was no longer considered as a guest.

The doctoral dissertation that finally made its way out of the Sociology Department at Michigan State University, "Social Strategies in Petty Production: Three Small-Scale Industries in Urban Sudan," was what I had come to Sudan to research. While serving as a Peace Corps Volunteer in neighboring Chad I came up with the idea that I would pursue academic African Studies when I returned home. Chad gave me an appreciation of the cultures of the Sahelian/Sudanic belt that crossed Africa from Senegal to Eritrea, and my Michigan State adviser recommended that I add an African language to my skills in planning a career as an African Studies professor. Arabic seemed like a good choice to go with the French-language skill I had developed in teaching high school in Chad, and Arabic combined with my interest in the Sahelian belt identified Sudan as a site for my dissertation research. I had also developed an interest in Sufism, an aspect of Islam often thought of as its mystical orientation, which further intensified the logic of going to Sudan. I considered Islam's presence in Africa to be rooted in Sufi teachings and organizations, no matter how far African Islam may have strayed from those roots, and Sudan had a rich Sufi history. As I learned more Arabic and prepared to go to Sudan, I decided that once there I would become a Sufi, although at the time I was not actually sure what that might entail. My time teaching at a lycée in rural Chad had left me feeling that I wanted a deeper experience in Africa, and that Sufism could be its vehicle.

This young man had so many agendas as he set out for Sudan! But the luxuries of youth, of having that generous Fulbright-Hays dissertation grant, of wanting to savor an African experience and not being in any particular hurry, meant that I was not anxious about the ordering of those agendas. I did have some anxiety, however, about my lack of proficiency in spoken Arabic, despite two years of study as part of my graduate course work. In fact, the greatest stomach cramp I have ever had grabbed me as my plane circled Khartoum Airport at the end of 1981, ready to deliver me into a land where I felt that I could not speak the language. And me with all those agendas.

My first few months in Sudan were spent observing work in Khartoum's small-scale industrial sites—where I intended to collect sociological data—and trying to learn Arabic. I discovered that Sudanese hospitality was a great help to my research in that the artisans in the workshops of my study—tailors, carpenters, metalworkers—had no objection to my hanging out in their shops, despite the fact that I was unable to tell them clearly what on earth I was doing there, and they usually offered me tea. These workshops were generally found in the "industrial sites" at the margins of the growing cities, housed in everything from sophisticated shops with showrooms to portable sewing-machine tables that could be moved from backs of trucks to the shade of a large tree. Any of these shops, particularly tailor shops, could also be found in residential areas. Tailors who specialized in women's clothing had shops that were convenient to their customers and accommodating to women's culture that restricted their movement beyond home to a great extent.

Studying the sociology of the urban worker did not necessarily offer me a chance to see where and how these workers lived in their homes, so when a tailor whose shop I had been hanging around invited me home to lunch I quickly accepted; I was also busy sampling Sudanese home cooking when I could. But I had woken that day feeling somewhat queasy and decided to carry on with my research figuring it was the heat getting to me. At lunchtime I walked with the tailor to his house nearby, and he sat me down in the saloon to wait. When the large tray was brought out by one of his younger brothers, other men in the family gathered around to share the meal. I crouched down with everyone and picked up a piece of bread to dip into one of the many sauces in front of me. I eyed the bread and noticed a small insect baked into it, hardly unusual but it did set my stomach off. I excused myself, ran out to the courtyard, and immediately vomited all over the entrance to the family toilet.

It turned out that I had malaria, which often announces itself with severe headache and vomiting. The sympathetic family put me to bed, where I stayed for a day or two, getting to see more of the inside of a tailor's house than I had planned.

In my spare time I had also begun my quest to find Sufis who would allow me to live with them and teach me how to become one. These encounters sometimes ended in disaster, usually the result of my still-developing Arabic. One Sufi group that invited me with an offer of a place to sleep became my standard of what to avoid. I sat on the bed that had been assigned to me in the corner of the *housh*, or courtyard, of the sheikh's house and watched as the small group of maybe six followers of this sheikh prayed the final three of the five daily prayers at one time so that they could commence an evening of drinking *aragi,* the home-brewed gin of choice in the area. The Qur'an warns that one should not pray while drunk, so these guys felt that they were sticking to the letter of that revelation while fulfilling a basic Muslim obligation.

Whatever their disposition toward Islamic principles, I was in awe of the unexpected hospitality offered by all these Sudanese willing to take in the wandering American. My first solo bus trip out of Khartoum was an excellent illustration of this welcome. I had wanted to make a weekend visit to a small village in the Gezira called Um Magad, to start to get a better idea of the rural roots of my urban workers. The village was on the west bank of the Blue Nile as it rushed north out of Ethiopia's highlands, joining the languid White Nile at Khartoum to make the main Nile. But because all of these mud-walled hamlets looked alike to me from the road, I mistakenly got off the bus one village south of my destination. I walked into the warren of walled compounds and asked the first man I saw if this was Um Magad. He didn't really answer me but gestured that I should follow him to his house. He sat me down in his saloon and disappeared, returning quickly with a large aluminum tray featuring a breakfast of *foul* (long-simmered fava beans), tomatoes, a fried egg, and bread. We ate in some degree of silence, or rather I ate and he watched me: it was a late hour for a farmer's breakfast. Finally he escorted me to the place where I had entered his village and he pointed in the direction of Um Magad, where I headed, most likely for another breakfast.

When I reached Um Magad after a short walk I was subjected to a logical and silent interrogation from villagers—very conventional Sudanese Muslims all—that I never experienced with any Republican brother. The old men of this Blue Nile village wanted to know how "Muslim" I really was. A few of them made a gesture miming the cutting off the tip of the index finger with the other index finger—and then gesturing "so?" with both hands as they anticipated a positive response from me. The Prophet's *sunna*, or personal practice, required that men be circumcised, and while this was standard practice for all Sudanese males, it was not an initiation question on the Republican list. The miming of the delicate question by the old village men rather than asking me directly was also an indicator of the sense that the questioners felt it was a somewhat rude question to begin with. The earnest desire of these older villagers to see me Muslim was confirmed by the frequency with which they would quietly stuff a Sudanese one-pound note into my shirt pocket or squeeze one into my hand discreetly. This was their way of congratulating me on my decision to embrace Islam; more *baraka* than I felt worthy of.

I remember that weekend in the Gezira as also getting me into more trouble as I tried to figure out customs related to the traditional garments that Sudanese men wore. The clothing that men wore under the jellabiya, the *arage* long shirt and baggy pants *sirwaal,* were also appropriate for sleeping and/or just hanging-out around the village. I visited this village, Um Magad, at the torrid height of the hot season, and the men invited me to join with them as they took a quick afternoon swim in the Blue Nile. As we reached the river bank, I noted with dread that everyone was swimming in their boxer-short-type underwear. I guess I thought of the long cotton billowy pants as underwear, so that was *all* that I was wearing! I gave my Arabic a good workout by trying to explain my dilemma to one of my hosts as we stood on the bank of the river, who of course calmly said *"mafi mushkila,"* no problem, and told me just to swim in the pants. So I floated along the Blue Nile with my pants inflated as water wings.

Although my Arabic vocabulary improved in interesting ways from that experience, I returned to my research focus and to getting to a point in the language where I could do interviews. An American friend who was teaching at the University of Khartoum where I was a research affiliate told me about a marvelous Sufi chanting, or *dhikir,* she had recently attended in Omdurman, the old city across the Nile from Khartoum, and how much I might enjoy that cultural exposure. She introduced me to Abdalla Ernest Johnson, an American who taught English language at the university and who had been a Republican Brother for several years. He took me to the dhikir that week before sunset on Thursday, when the Republicans gathered for one of their major meetings of the week at the home of their leader, Ustadh (teacher) Mahmoud Mohamed Taha.

Abdalla joined the semicircle of brothers and sisters who stood chanting the name of God in the declining sun outside of the house. The dhikir was intense, led by a brother with a big voice who had been appointed by Ustadh Mahmoud, and followed by the rest of the group of about fifty, strongly repeating over and over, some swaying in rhythm to the act of remembering the name of God, the meaning of dhikir. Others stood straight in intense concentration of the simple phrasing, as if repeating and absorbing the name of God might instantly transport them somewhere else. I stood off to the side barely resisting the rhythm, behind Ustadh Mahmoud who oversaw the group of chanting brothers and sisters standing next to the blue door to his house made of *jalous,* the mud construction material common in this region by the river Nile.

The chanting ended with a resounding *Allah!* and with Ustadh Mahmoud blessing the whole group with the phrase, *Allah yafizkum* (may God keep you) just before the call to the sunset prayer, *al-mughrib.* Like the chanting ritual, the Republican call to prayer had its own modernist and dramatic riff. In my few months in Khartoum of trying to get to a point where I could converse in Arabic, I had discovered that the *azan,* or call to prayer, was a most useful language teaching tool. Azan is called out from mosques all over the city five times a day, the same ancient, prescribed pledges over and over (except for the early morning azan, which includes the wonderful line, "prayer is better than sleep"). And the azan's words are clearly enunciated in song. I found that by figuring out the meaning of the words to the azan, I could begin to take the sentences apart and string them into other contexts. So, for example, while weaving the first early morning azan phrase "prayer is better than sleep" into conversations would only produce amusement, there were infinite uses for my new knowledge of the comparative grammatical construction "better than" (*kheirun min . . .*).

As my Arabic improved, I noticed a sharp increase in my own invocation of the name of God. There seemed to be an expression praising the Almighty for everything from completing a bath or haircut to starting a car, or commencing or finishing a meal. God was more ever-present in my life as it was voiced in Arabic than He had ever been in English.

Back at my first dhikir, the Republican Sisters filed inside Ustadh Mahmoud's house for the sunset prayer while the brothers rolled out long straw mats on which to pray in the empty lot to the west of the building. Abdalla presented me to Ustadh Mahmoud, who said something about inviting me to lunch in a couple of days. He was not a tall man, but stood very straight for a man of seventy-something, dressed in the simple white cotton arage shirt and sirwal pants that were the comfortable everyday standard. I participated in the sunset prayer, went through a round of warm handshakes while collecting some new Arabic greetings, and then made my way back across the Nile to Khartoum where I stayed in a flat that Michigan State University had rented for medical researchers. I stayed there for free as the well-educated night watchman.

I was excited to return to Omdurman as soon as possible for my meeting with Ustadh Mahmoud, so Abdalla arranged for us to lunch with him two days later, on Saturday afternoon. We arrived at the blue door, and I was ushered into the ordinary and small house that was crowded with a multigenerational group of brothers and sisters performing a variety of tasks for the organization, or just wanting to be near their teacher. We met with Ustadh Mahmoud in his small bedroom/study, containing a single *angareb,* a bed of rope and wood, and several bookcases crowded with tomes in Arabic and scientific artifacts, like smooth stones and seashells. There were decorated verses of the Qur'an on the wall and a small table and two chairs. Ustadh sat on the bed and we took the chairs. He asked me to explain what I was looking for in Sudan, and I gave him a quick and simple half English/half Arabic review that primarily focused on my research and why I had selected Sudan for my study. I didn't say to him, "I want to be a Sufi," but that was what I was thinking as I told him of my spiritual interests in Sudan. Over our lunch of the thin flat sorghum crepe-like bread *kisra* and a vegetarian version of the wild okra stew *um rigayga* ("mother of the thin hair" for its stringy-okra consistency), his most memorable words to me that afternoon were, "We have no formal initiation ceremony in the Republican Brotherhood, and you are welcome to join us and see what we are about." I found this significant in that my reading about some Sufi orders had taught me about the recruitment and elaborate induction processes that included pledging obedience and loyalty to the sheikh and other rituals. He was not effusive with me, but certainly cordial and interested. I thanked Ustadh Mahmoud for lunch—he was a teacher to his followers, not a Sufi sheikh—and returned to Khartoum to think about how involved I wanted to get with Ustadh and his followers.

When I first met Mahmoud Mohamed Taha in early 1982 he had been focusing on his work to spread his idea of an Islam for contemporary times for more than forty years. He transmitted a message of tolerance and equality that he felt was the only way for Islam to be practiced under the conditions created by a modern, changing, and dangerous world. Sudan in Africa was the locus of his life's work. Omer El Garrai remembered Taha saying, "I am an African. I like the night, the scent of *buhur* (incense), the hot weather." In his book *Religion and Social Development* Taha wrote, "Africa is the first home of Man. In it his life appeared at the beginning and in its freedom will be achieved at the end."[1] Taha had a dark complexion; the color called *azraq* (dark blue) by the Sudanese, and he bore the traditional facial scars of his Rikabiya ethnic group, a people with origins in the far north of the country. Although the African and Arab heritage of Sudan has been a significant factor in Sudanese politics, one Republican friend told me that Taha had said, "We are black or Negro. We are not Arab but our Mother Tongue is Arabic. We inherited values from both Arab and Negro." This kind of thinking was also trouble in Sudan, roiled by its complex Afro-Arab identity issues. The quarters opposing Ustadh Mahmoud, it occurred to me, were also the ones engaged in the suppression of Sudan's African identity. Taha's work as a religious reformer was preceded by his participation in the effort to secure Sudan's political independence as a republic, a period of time in which he also became known to the British colonial authorities as a troublemaker.

Mahmoud Mohamed Taha did not have a rigorous religious education. In the 1930s Taha studied engineering at Gordon Memorial College, which until 1944 was Sudan's only government secondary school, later to become the University of Khartoum. Young men studied at Gordon College in order to provide skilled manpower for the colonial administration. He was employed by Sudan Railways for two years, working for various lengths of time in Kassala and eastern Sudan, and Atbara. He also joined the Graduates Congress, the Gordon College alumni group that was the crucible for Sudan's independence struggle.

The Graduates Congress was established in 1938, two years after Taha's graduation, with an idea of the Indian Congress in mind, according to Ahmed Khair, one of its early leaders.[2] The Graduates Congress stimulated the nationalist activism that fueled the move to independence from the Anglo-Egyptian Condominium that ruled Sudan. Political parties were spawned by the Graduates' efforts, with many of them maintaining ties to either colonial patronage or the traditional Sufi sects. Taha's vision at that time was of the establishment of a *Republic* of Sudan, a political entity not yet existing in an Arabic-speaking country. Other Sudan parties pushed for either integration under the Egyptian crown or hereditary religious rule under the Mahdi family. Taha and ten colleagues, all employees of the colonial government, founded the Republican Party in October 1945 to work toward an independent republic. Taha was elected chairman at its first meeting.[3] While the group considered its small size and discussed forming a coalition with one of its rivals, the Ummah Party of the Mahdists, a vote was taken and the consensus was against such a move. Omer El Garrai had told me that Ustadh Mahmoud had explained to him that initially the majority had wanted to join the bigger party, but the discussion yielded a decision to the contrary. El Garrai said that Ustadh Mahmoud told him, "If we had decided otherwise, you wouldn't be here with me today." Ustadh Mahmoud's point was that if the much larger Ummah Party had absorbed the Republicans their identity would have been lost.

The small group that had rallied around Ustadh Mahmoud's principles decided against making other alliances because they felt that neither political Islamism nor secularism were solutions for Sudan's problems. The Republican Party manifesto, *Ghul: Hathihi Sibeeli* (Say: this is my path!), a title with a distinctly Qur'anic ring, detailed a civil society rooted in Islam and the Qur'an.[4] The large parties, the Ummah and the Democratic Unionists—both had religious roots and overtones in their rhetoric, but no specific Islamic agenda at that point in the independence struggle. Mahmoud Mohamed Taha wrote a letter describing his politics in 1963 to then Harvard doctoral researcher John Voll that was prescient with concerns that would overtake Sudan decades later.

> My own party was "The Republican Party." It built its ideology on Islam. We opposed the tendencies of some of the political parties towards an Islamic state because we were sure they did not know what they were talking about. An Islamic state built on ignorance of the pure facts of Islam can be more detrimental to progress than a secular state of average ability. Religious fanaticism is inalienable from religious ignorance. . . . The Republican Party was the most explicit party in outlining a program for the formation of an Islamic state—only we did not call it Islamic. We were aiming at universality, because universality is the order of the day. Only the universal contents were tapped.[5]

Ahmad Khair of the Graduates Congress wrote about the Republican Party in the midst of Sudan's struggle for independence. "The men of the Republican Party proved their true will and the strength of their belief, and that is why they enjoy the respect of all. Their leader proved to have sincerity, power and resilience. It is perhaps these reasons, in addition to their different objectives, that caused them to stand alone and in isolation."[6]

In 1946 Mahmoud Mohamed Taha and several members of his party were arrested by the colonial administration for unlawful political activities—they had been handing out anticolonial leaflets—and were sentenced to one year in prison, becoming Sudan's first political prisoners of the independence movement. Republican Party members agitated for their colleagues' release, and the group left prison after fifty days. Taha was back in prison after two months for leading a demonstration to protest the arrest of a woman, Alminein Hakim, in Rufa'a for the circumcision of her daughter, Fayza, an incident which became an emblem of Taha's spiritual philosophy of human development and its implications for women; it was a story that was told to me many times by many different Republican brothers and sisters. And it was a story with implications for Taha's intentions of putting his ideas into action.

In response to a markedly paternalistic public outcry in Britain, the colonial authority "added Section 284A to the Sudan Penal Code forbidding the practice of a severe type of female circumcision known as Pharaonic circumcision."[7] My own reading of the colonial documents was that the public attitude in Britain was driven more by the sensational aspect of the cultural practice than by any genuine concern for women's and girls' health. And all over colonized Africa, the "native question" was debated with conflicts over legal actions taken by colonial governments and the perception of the colonized as to whether the prohibited activities were in fact their legitimate rights. Yusif Lotfi, one of the younger brothers of Taha's wife told me that he had understood from

22

Ustadh Mahmoud that the British had imposed the law to bring to the world's attention how "primitive" Sudan was, not yet fit for independence. Mahmoud Mohamed Taha organized his historic protest after Friday prayers in Rufa'a, his hometown, an incident reported by a District Officer of the British colonial government:

> The Hassaheissa-Rufa'a disturbances, of which we have not yet received full reports, came as a complete surprise. They were indicative, however, of what is to be expected when a few fanatics find grounds for stirring up an irresponsible town population which is already undermined by anti-government vernacular press and propaganda. In this case it was very bad luck that Mohammed Mahmud Taher [sic], the fanatic leader of the Republican party [sic] and bitter opponent of the female circumcision reforms should be living in the very town where the first trial of an offence against the circumcision laws happened to take place. The case [i.e., against the woman] was quashed on no other grounds than lack of evidence.[8]

Mahmoud Mohamed Taha, his political organization and subsequent spiritual movement and followers, opposed the ancient pre-Islamic practice of female circumcision and did not practice it in their families for the most part. Taha's point in organizing the Rufa'a protest of the woman's arrest for circumcising her daughter was that the British could not legislate Sudanese morality and that such laws were unsustainable in a country where women were not given access to religious training, education, or social status that would empower them to end the practice themselves. Taha made his point that the arrested woman who had performed the circumcision stood for all Sudanese women by referring to her in the Rufa'a demonstration as "our sister, our mother, our wife"; this was a spiritual test for Ustadh Mahmoud. Ironically, Mohamed Mahmoud (not related to Taha), writing in 2001, continues to miss Taha's point and demonstrates how difficult it has been over fifty years for Taha to reach his countrymen and women with his message that their understanding of Islam must change. Mohamed Mahmoud wrote, "Taha's act of defiance against British law in this incident contributed the single greatest damage to the welfare of Sudanese women";[9] that is, Mohamed Mahmoud perceived Mahmoud Mohamed Taha to be demonstrating in support of female circumcision. Sudan today continues to have one of the highest rates of female circumcision in the world despite decades-old laws banning the practice. The Sudanese human rights lawyer and activist Dr. Asma Abdel Halim pointed out to me in 2003 that the *sayyidain,* the two leaders of the largest traditional political organizations in Sudan, the Ummah Party and the Democratic Unionists, did nothing to urge their many followers to heed the British law of the 1940s, did not say anything about it in public, or even stop the practice in their own families. Taha's own campaign against female circumcision could be perceived as counterintuitive, if we were to rely solely on liberal Western analysis and postcolonial hindsight. But the incident does provide an example of the quality of the long-term spiritual goals that were central to Taha's movement: difficult to implement and not immediately or unanimously adopted by his followers, but highly principled and consistent with his overall thinking about how human society could and should evolve. Taha was at once taking a stand against colonial imposition of cultural authority and for improving the status of women through education so that they might speak up on their own behalf against such "dangerous traditional practices."

As pre-independence politics developed, it became clear that an independent Sudan would be ruled by one of the sectarian parties, either the Umma Party of the Mahdists or the Democratic Unionist Party of the Khatmiya Sufi tariqa-Mirghani family. When he was released from prison after two years, Mahmoud Mohamed Taha retreated from politics to his home region of

Rufa'a, a market town on the east bank of the Blue Nile in the heart of Sufi Sudan. There he continued with the *khalwa,* the self-imposed spiritual retreat ritual that he had started in prison. Taha's brother-in-law Ali Lotfi told me in 1999 that Ustadh Mahmoud practiced the *samadi* fast in prison for twenty-nine days, which is a total fast from eating and drinking. According to Ali, the British authorities did not believe that anyone could actually fast so completely so they weighed his bath water before and after to see if he was drinking the water. Taha emerged from his isolation in 1951 and rededicated his political organization to Islamic revival renaming it the New Islamic Mission (*al dawa al-islamiya al-jadida*). The Republican Brotherhood (*al-akhwaan al jumhoureen*) became the group's popular label, a name that also acknowledged the continuity of the spiritual message that had been part of Taha's political party. I'll note that the gendered concept of "brotherhood" in Sudanese Arabic does incorporate both men and women, where it is also common for a woman to address a mixed group as "akhwan," that is, brothers and sisters in faith.

On January 1, 1956, Sudan became an independent republic under Prime Minister Ismail al-Azhari of the National Unionist Party. The original Republican Party itself was dissolved along with all other political parties by the coup of Jaafar Nimeiry in 1969.

Ustadh Mahmoud and his followers prayed deeply and sincerely, held fast to the Prophet's Sunna, worked hard to make their country better, and cared for each other. Although this may not appear at variance with accepted Sudanese Islamic norms— the country is full of people being "good Muslims"—the Republicans lived their lives in a modest manner and in a public atmosphere, in earnest demonstration of what effort it took, what discipline was required to lead a life moving progressively closer to God, achieving unity (*towhid*). While the goal was to insert a love of God deeply within them, the station en route to that destination was a public manifestation of Islam's possibilities. Their devoted work to demonstrating to their country and the world that Islam could be a modern spiritual experience was—most importantly—strengthening their own personal convictions of that goal. Their understanding of the Qur'an's message is what the Republicans called "new," not the knowledge itself. They expressed that understanding with the expression, *"kalam gadim, fahm jaded"* (old words, new understanding).

Much of what I learned and remembered from the brothers and sisters about Ustadh Mahmoud and his teachings was in the form of stories. One story illustrates the personal transformation that was central to the Republican approach to Islam. A Sufi follower of Ustadh Mahmoud visited a *wali*, or holy man, in his tomb in the eastern Gezira village of Tundub, a well-known center of Sufi learning that was a dusty speck on the wide *butana* (plain). The Sufi told the wali that he was on his way to visit Ustadh Mahmoud in Omdurman and asked if there was anything that the wali would like to present to Ustadh. A hand quickly came out of the tomb holding a *sibha,* a set of carved wooden prayer beads common to Sufi practice, which the Sufi then took as a gift to his teacher in Omdurman. When he presented the beads to Ustadh Mahmoud, the teacher said, "This is a wonderful present, but take the beads back to your wali and tell him that Ustadh Mahmoud wants something greater." The Sufi dutifully returned to Tundub with the beads, went directly to the tomb, and when he told the wali of Ustadh Mahmoud's request, the hand came out and snatched back the beads, with nothing to offer in their place.

When the Sufi reported what had transpired in the wali's tomb to Ustadh Mahmoud, the latter replied, "Your wali has not replaced the prayer beads with a superior gift because he knows that you now follow the Republican ideology and that there is nothing greater than that."

My experience at the front line of Islamic social change was often contextualized through these stories. As Republicans recount tales such as that of the Sufi gift, they are describing for me the intimate understanding that Mahmoud Mohamed Taha had of his followers' spiritual origins and what he had to do to nudge them gently down an improved path, the meaning of Sunna. The cumulative impact of these stories constitutes a form of contemporary hagiography of this Sudanese Islamic leader. In the story reported above Taha recognizes the wali's role in the Sufi's life and used it to reorient the Sufi's spiritual goals, what Ustadh Mahmoud did in effect every day with his followers at their meetings. The several versions of this Sufi gift story that have been told to me—each with a slightly different pedagogical point—represent the willingness of Ustadh Mahmoud's followers to make intelligent responses to their teacher's guidance, to engage in dialogue with his teachings. His followers fell on a continuum of attachment to their Sufi pasts—every Muslim Sudanese has some connection to Sufism either through family or direct practice. When I asked one brother if he had a version of this particular story he told me, "We have the original guy [in Ustadh Mahmoud]. Why should I bother with that *darwish* [i.e., a follower of a traditional Sufi master]?" Mahmoud Mohamed Taha subjected Sufism to a critical review, but he did not dismiss it violently, accepting what was strong within Sufism. An obvious point though in this story is the symbolism of the sibha. Prayer beads, while very common to Sufi religious practice, are in fact considered by some contemporary Muslims to be *bida*, or an innovation emerging in Islam after the life of the Prophet. In other words, the prayer beads themselves represent an Islam that was not part of the Prophet Mohamed's own personal practice or Sunna.

Mahmoud Mohamed Taha's unwavering consistency, from his perspective on the female circumcision issue which he said would be resolved only through the elevation of the nation's consciousness of women, through his forty-year steadfast position opposing the proposal to unify Sudan with Egypt, to the damning leaflet that condemned President Jaafar Nimeiry's "Islamic laws" as "distorting Islam, humiliating the People and jeopardizing national unity," which led to his execution in 1985—all characterized Taha's link of Islam with freedom and personal development in a unique contemporary African context. His consistency was also the natural result of his complete lack of hypocrisy.

In a lecture at Ohio University in 2001, the Sudanese journalist and scholar Abdalla Gallab suggested contrasting this Republican focus on an educated mission to revive Islam with their most significant rivals and the most dominant political force in Sudan for the past three decades, the Sudan branch of the Muslim Brotherhood. Muslim Brothers drew their strength in Sudan from their commerce and trading activities and their international ties, their taking advantage of the new wealth brought on by the early 1970s oil boom in the Gulf, and from the black market currency trade. The Republicans' focus was on the intellectual development of its membership and on maintaining a Sufi-influenced modest lifestyle. The Republicans tended to sacrifice material gain for mind-expanding pursuits—education, degrees, learning, travel, and spending time with each other—all of which better prepared them to absorb Mahmoud Mohamed Taha's complex theology.

The Republican brothers and sisters' self-conscious practice of faith was to lead to the transformation of themselves and their society. Women were not excluded from this process; in fact, they were an important focus of the Republican ideology and all of its activities. Women's improved status within the community was an indicator of Republican success. Their voices were strong at the meetings and even in the call to prayer. Women's roles were sources of pride to the Republicans and of controversy in the wider society. Giving voice to an articulate vision of Islam was the duty of every Republican brother and sister. Those voices were trained in the movement's many communication campaigns: books and pamphlets, newspaper writings, and public speaking events.

For me, the importance of this movement lies in the sincere application of its sanctioned words in the actual daily lives of its followers. In their words and deeds the Republicans provided an alternative to extremism and violence in the name of Islam, to intolerance, to the sectarianism that had deeply divided Sudan, and to the denial of women's rights under the pretext of adherence to Islamic values. In that the Republicans had all been brought up in a culture marked by patriarchy and paternalism, the Republican path to progress was always a challenge.

I chose to work in Sudan because of its Sufi history, and the Republicans helped me better understand those roots; they maintained a deep respect for the Sufi gnosis that described the relationship between Man and God. But Republicans were selective in what contribution Sufism could make to a faith for today's world. Theirs was not a different Islam but one in which faith and their understanding of its required actions were brought as close together as they thought humanly possible. This great effort, or methodology of faith, is what the Republicans took from the Sufi tradition. The Republicans practiced a local Islam with aspirations to something much larger—local not in the sense of provincial but as a consequence of its economic and political limitations. The themes and ideas expounded upon by the men and women of this movement emerged from their analysis of world events and their understanding of God's purpose for them. The dominant aspect of the local was that this all took place in an intimate atmosphere and that they were not a large movement, numbering about two thousand families at the movement's height, roughly in the decade 1975–85. To be a Republican, in effect, was to know and to want to know personally every other Republican, an intense solidarity.

This was a local Islam in that it was deliberately, consistently, and carefully lived in a specific place with a culture and a history.

A central part of the Republican message was that Islam *was* in the right place and the right time, that Islam was eternally contemporary. Although the Republicans found themselves in constant conflict with other local constructions of Islam in Sudan, they offered theirs as the universal, not a utopia. But coalitions and compromise were also not on their agenda, nor were dialogues with other moderate approaches to Islamic reform, except as these approaches were brought in through the experiences of those seeking Republican membership. The Republicans were not trying to move the clock backward; indeed, the ambitious Republican goal was to move it forward to the point where Islam could meet its millenarian destiny in transforming all of humanity, what Ustadh Mahmoud viewed as the ultimate liberation. In his dedication of the first edition of his signature book, *The Second Message of Islam* (1967), Mahmoud Mohamed Taha wrote, "Good tidings it is that God has in store for us such perfection of intellectual and emotional life as no eye has ever seen, no ear has ever heard, and has never occurred to any human being."[10]

The millenarian dimension of Republican thought was a subtle theme and focused on by the membership with varying degrees of intensity and at different times in movement history. Its focus on the return of the Messiah to Earth and bringing a reign of a thousand years of peace was one of the exotic mysteries that stuck in my Western mind as I listened to Republican debates. But as al-Karsani states, "Millennialism has always been present in Islam as one of the 'means of expressing dissatisfaction with the state of society,' . . . 'when the Islamic community has felt an imminent danger to its world of value and meaning.'"[11] Ustadh Mahmoud chose the 97th chapter of the Qur'an, *Qadr*, as the anthem for the group, which was read/chanted collectively as the opening and closing prayer for all of Republican gatherings. The chapter, "The Night of Power," is a short one, commonly one of the first to be committed to memory by Muslims worldwide, and reads:

We have indeed revealed this (message) in the Night of
Power: And what will explain to them what the Night of
Power is? The Night of Power is better than a thousand
Months. Therein come down the angels and the Spirit by
God's permission, on every errand! Peace!. . . This until the
rise of Morn! (Yusuf Ali translation)

The verse refers to the night during the holy month of Ramadan when the Prophet Mohamed first began to receive the
revelation of the Qur'an from the Angel Gabriel. The reference
to "a thousand months" is one of the many clues in the Qur'an
to the coming time of Peace. Ustadh Mahmoud said the chapter
was like a "sister" to all of the Republicans, indicating the importance of its message.

I had about a year and a half in the presence of Mahmoud
Mohamed Taha—seeing him on a daily basis—before he was
taken to detention and prison for the final time. But his followers were my agents for his message, and I lived closely with
them in Sudan and have continued to do so for more than thirty
years, all over the world. As much as possible in a personal story
framed by social science convention, this book tries to represent the Republican Brotherhood as its members have expressed
and interpreted for me in interviews and conversations how they
wish to be represented, through their words, ideas, books, lectures, hymns, and memories. This book is also a product of
their cooperation and of the methodological orientation that
suggests that we are part of what we seek to understand. The anthropologist Richard Werbner describes the "rights of recount-
ability"—"the right, especially in the face of state violence and
oppression, to make a citizen's memory known and acknowledged in the public sphere."[12] Republican engagement of public
culture in Sudan and their rethinking of the life cycle's basic
rituals in infant-naming ceremonies, weddings, and funerals
provided opportunities for many of the brothers and sisters to

express to me the reasons why their Republican approach was an improvement in the way Islam could be practiced. Indeed, while many Republicans want the world to know about their teacher, his teachings, and about the possibilities for humanity provided in Islam, there were others in the movement who maintained the view that there was no need to explain anything to anyone on the outside. As one senior leader of the movement told my friend Mustafa El-Jaili while speaking about a foreign researcher (not me) who had expressed interest in the movement, "The world will come to us when they see what we are accomplishing here. But if his study helps *him* to understand this knowledge of Islam better, then that is fine."

My interactions with the Republican intellectual community were essential to my understanding the subtle link between Republican thought and progressive action, as well as that between voice and authority. More important is the issue of voice as the Republicans re-represent themselves in the Sudan of today—thirty-plus years after the execution of Mahmoud Mohamed Taha. One of my mentors in this group—speaking truth to power without pause—has been Abdullahi Ahmed An-Na'im, professor of law at Emory University. As a lawyer and scholar of human rights, Dr. Abdullahi has developed a professional field that closely resonates to the work of his teacher, Mahmoud Mohamed Taha. In Dr. Abdullahi's published work or in his speaking engagements around the world, he acknowledges the role that Mahmoud Mohamed Taha played in his spiritual and intellectual development. However, in the Western media, the names Abdullahi Ahmed An-Na'im and Mahmoud Mohamed Taha are often confused, to the consternation of some and great surprise to those in Sudan, who know explicitly that Abdullahi is not seeking the mantle of Ustadh Mahmoud. Another prominent Republican teacher, Ustadh Khalid El Haj, a retired school administrator in Rufa'a, articulates the problem of representation with utmost respect when he said in an interview about a book he published in 2006, *Peace in Islam*, "I am *talmith* [a pupil] of Ustadh Mahmoud, not directed by him." No one has been appointed or has sought to succeed Mahmoud Mohamed Taha in his role of spiritual guide, teacher of the movement, although Republican brothers and sisters in Sudan have been able to meet freely and frequently for the last few years for spiritual purposes. The charisma was never routinized.

Abdullahi Ahmed An-Na'im wrote thirty years ago:

> Is it possible that Ustadh Mahmoud's work will be completely forgotten in a few years, without having a lasting impact? I do not think so. Whatever the Muslims may think of the answers, he has no doubt raised fundamental and searching questions. . . . More important, I would submit, is his personal example of commitment and courage. To have pursued his goals so selflessly and consistently for forty years, especially through his own personal life-style, is an exceptional achievement. The example of this single man's living for and by his convictions, more than dying for them, is truly inspiring not only to Muslims but to all the people of the world.[13]

It is important for me to consider how the Republican men and women understood the theological streams that flowed through their writings and lived them and taught them to their children both in Sudan and in exile. My memories are complemented by conversations with more than forty Republican brothers and sisters between 1996 and 2010 conducted in Sudan, Egypt, England, Ireland, the Netherlands, Qatar, the United Arab Emirates, and the United States. Republicans have joined the "digital Islam" community, so their words in email communications have been available to me as well. In many of these conversations individual Republicans recall the words of Ustadh Mahmoud. I have checked these quotes with other Republicans in each case, which in turn invariably led to more memories, with subtle differences but never significant disagreement. Memories of Ustadh Mahmoud are passed around by Republicans like a valuable goblet full of a life-giving elixir that should not be spilled or a drop wasted. My task here is to interpret what I saw and heard and try to provide some context for the Western reader. Although many have encouraged me to write this book, no Republican brother or sister has actually authorized it on behalf of the movement, nor does such an authority exist. The gaps in my knowledge will appear profound to my Sudanese friends, and I hope those gaps provide a good jumping-off point for the next book on the Republican Brotherhood.

Ustadh Mahmoud frequently said, "All Republicans are teachers," a condition that made easier my task as a student of their approach to Islam. I remember an early experience with my friend Abdel Gadir, who had worked a lifetime as a primary school teacher and then school-inspector, which illustrated Republican capacity to instruct while constructing a coherent philosophy of life. We were taking a walk on the high bank of the Blue Nile near his house in Rufa'a at *asur*, the late afternoon time of day when the sun colors the world ochre. As we made our way across the dried *tummy*, the Gezira cracking clay that made the region so fertile, a man quickly approached from the other direction, his white arage shirt flapping in the wind. Abdel Gadir loved to help me develop my Arabic vocabulary, particularly for things colloquial or unique to his region. I called it my "grandmother's vocabulary" (*mufradat al-huboobat*). He poked me and pointed to the oncoming figure saying, "Steve, *da shnu?* [What is that?]" I cringed, thinking that I was about to learn the local derogatory term for the mentally handicapped in that I knew the approaching man, Hussein, had that condition from birth. Abdel Gadir ignored my shrug and answered his own question, "He is a darwish!"

I found his reference to the Sufi mystics who inhabited the cemeteries and tombs of holy men both simple and startling. In one word Abdel Gadir had paid Hussein a tribute. To be darwish—a person dedicated completely to remembering God—was a status to which Abdel Gadir himself could aspire and, in the meantime, respect. By describing Hussein as darwish Abdel Gadir accepted Hussein as he was, in fact saw what was God-like within him and made room in his community for him, using "darwish" as a common local euphemism for mentally handicapped that was also inclusive. The Republicans saw the world through Islam's possibilities rather than through the controlling or limiting functions of religion in society. That progress in global Islam could start on the banks of the Blue Nile was a Republican given. That the world should know more about these courageous people is the purpose of this book.

2

The Path of the Prophet

To be a Republican Brother required considerable time and stamina. The work to sustain the movement fell particularly hard on the *azaba,* the single men members of the movement who lived near Mahmoud Mohamed Taha's house in Omdurman. They were expected to attend all of the meetings, beginning with an early morning session at dawn, take a significant role in the production and distribution of Republican Brotherhood literature, attend the various lectures and community events associated with a social movement that was also at the center of its members' lives, and of course, work hard at being better Muslims. The Republican movement was intense at this stage of its history and many of the young brothers got little sleep. No one objected to this demanding schedule, in fact the credo of the bachelor group could have been "service with a smile." Brothers felt that spending as much time as possible with each other both offered an excellent opportunity to learn more about the Republican ideology and prevented them from going astray.

However, after a few months of complete immersion in the Republican way of life, I needed to come up for air. I felt that I was suffocating under the pressure of participating in every meeting; I was not spending enough time on my doctoral research. I may have also reflected on many conversations during my graduate studies about researchers "going native" and the impact that might have on one's data collection. I sought an appointment with Ustadh Mahmoud and went to see him at his house. It was unusual for one of the brothers or sisters to see Ustadh Mahmoud alone. There was both a sense in the community that no one should have any secrets from anyone else and also that if Ustadh Mahmoud said something significant, there should be another witness. Nevertheless, I was feeling that my "Western outlook" needed to take charge of my life in Sudan, and I wanted to carve out more time for myself. I am sure that I also felt, despite my earlier expressed desire for the Sufi life, that I was succumbing to the demands of Sudanese patriarchal culture. I was uncomfortable with customs like seeking "permission" from the senior brothers to go somewhere or do something.

I was apprehensive as I went into my meeting with Ustadh Mahmoud because I knew that I really did not know what I was going to say to him; I guess I was looking for some kind of guidance. Or at least, I wanted him to know me better. My impressions of the teacher were largely wrought through what I had understood about him from the brothers' conversations. Their devotion to him and their absolute commitment to his vision of Islam were palpable in everything that they did and said about him. The most often used introductory phrase I heard around the brothers' house where I lived was *"gaal al-Ustadh . . ."* ("Ustadh said . . . "). And the intense discussions of the *fikr jumhuriya,* the Republican ideology, at every meeting were leaving me behind. I could not read Ustadh Mahmoud's seminal work, *The Second Message of Islam,* which had not yet been translated into English. In fact, I was frequently asked if I had read the book and what I thought about it, and was also given impromptu tutorials on different aspects of it. But I dreaded the quiz.

Ustadh Mahmoud sat on his bed as he listened to me begin to seek permission for a looser affiliation with the brotherhood. As I launched into an explanation of my doctoral research, I suddenly felt silly and inarticulate, that my request was mundane next to the lofty spiritual goals of his movement. Ustadh Mahmoud's response to me made it clear that I had not succeeded in convincing him of the importance of my work in Sudan. He told me that I was welcome to live with the brothers for as long as I wanted. He continued to say that sometime soon the world would come to realize that the Republican ideology was what would deliver peace in our modern times. I had the sense that he was at once chiding me and implying that I had an amazing opportunity to be part of a critical event for humanity. I also began to understand the importance of guidance and advice as one trod the challenging spiritual path advocated by Ustadh Mahmoud.

He confirmed my feeling by announcing to the brothers and sisters at that evening's *jelsa* (meeting) at his house that they were to leave me alone. Happily for me, while that was surely an odd request, it was hardly in the Sudanese nature to ignore someone who lived in their midst. So I soon forgot about my awkward meeting with Ustadh Mahmoud. What I did do was try to become better informed about the ideology that motivated this movement, which is what I should have done in the first place.

Many of the brothers told me of a basic Republican philosophy that they had learned from Ustadh Mahmoud. He taught them that one's mind, words, and deeds all must be in sync; in other words, that it was essential that your thoughts, words and actions be linked in a unity of purpose. And that purpose, ultimately, was peace. I appreciated how this perspective was usually communicated to me visually by the speaker of this mantra gently touching his or her head, lips, and heart to indicate the connections. It sounded easy enough, reminding me initially of California New Age feel-good spirituality. But I quickly realized that this was a very serious, scripturally based behavioral methodology that the collective of the Republican brothers and sisters worked on together, checking and encouraging each other in its practice and on improving it. It was a challenging method to stick to, and with the brothers I frequently observed that there was even a competitive element to succeeding in strengthening one's practice. I observed, tried to practice, but managed to stay out of the competition, part of my strategy of trying not to draw attention to myself. I was emphatic about being in Sudan to learn and never be in the position of the all-knowing *khabir ajanabi* ("foreign expert") who had descended on Sudan to impart knowledge. The khabir ajanabi was actually a set character from Egyptian/Sudanese films and soap operas whose role came up when discussing foreigners who actually did not know enough to be very useful to the local circumstances—not a role I wanted to play in Sudan.

Mahmoud Mohamed Taha's vision for humankind was soaring. His sources included an amalgam of mystical reflection, deep knowledge and understanding of the Qur'an, and immersion in study of the life of the Prophet Mohamed, not unlike what many of the Muslim thinkers associated with Sufism had done in the past. But Ustadh Mahmoud's vision also came out of his own life experience, exposure to modern education and the difficult challenges of Sudan's independence struggle. Although Ustadh Mahmoud and the Republicans were careful to distinguish between themselves and the "conventional Sufis," there was certainly something mystical to his methods of concentration on prayer and on the Qur'an that led to the unity of his thinking and action. Progressive improvement in the practice of prayer and in being a Republican was always the intention.

"Unity," *al-towhid,* or "monotheism," was the concept and the goal very much at the center of the Republican ideology as communicated by Mahmoud Mohamed Taha. It was at once beautifully simple and utterly complex. As I tried to wrestle with it, I grew to understand that the complexity of the Republican message was what kept many Sudanese from joining the Republican Brotherhood. I was raised a Boston Catholic and the external simplicity of Islam is what initially attracted me to the faith. To profess Islam one simply recites as a believer the core *shahada*, or "witness," that there is No God But God and Mohamed Is His Prophet (*la ilaha l'allah wa Mohamdun rasulullah*). And then I was moved by visits to small villages along the Blue Nile where I had watched very old men take it upon themselves to demonstrate prayer to me, performing their ablutions while balancing on one crouched foot, and then falling from a standing position to their knees in a graceful motion, touching their foreheads to the ground in prayer. Shahada and prayer were the essences of Muslim life, and many deeply believing people in Sudan felt that it should not be more complicated than that, that no one should be in possession of "secret knowledge" of God's ways; no one should have to explain Islam to the true believer.

But the critical point of the Republican movement was that in order to promote and practice the Islam left to us by the Prophet Mohamed in these modern times, we must delve deeply into the meaning of the Qur'an and instruct ourselves, or reinstruct ourselves, in the path of Islam followed by the Prophet himself. Humankind had become distracted, and it was time to restore the Path of the Prophet as the way a Muslim worships God, while never losing sight of the goal of self-actualization.

Because of the careful instruction and warm socialization of the brotherhood I had found in Omdurman, I decided that I would follow this particular path to Islam. I chose this group more on the basis of my rapid inclusion initially than, I would have to admit, on being convinced of the power or veracity of its message. I often thought about how my knowledge of Arabic and Islam were developing as they would in a Sudanese childhood—through social learning—and I spent time trying to understand this process. But I also quickly became aware that my choice of the Republicans was a controversial one in Sudan, that there were competing platforms for the Muslim soul. I needed to learn more about why I was satisfied with my choice to join these educated, progressive, welcoming people, and why that choice would make many Muslim activists in Sudan angry.

I also frequently reflected on my decision to embrace Islam, which, considering who I was and where I had come from, was probably more significant than my choice of following Ustadh Mahmoud. There is an expectation from childhood in Muslim culture that families will teach their children verses of the Qur'an, which they will commit to memory. Many children compete in festive tournaments where they exhibit how much they have memorized and/or the quality of their *tajweed*, or recitation, skills. The first chapter that I memorized was *al-Ikhlas*, "Sincerity," which is the chapter that virtually all Muslims have memorized because of its brevity. It reads in translation,

> Say: He is Allah, The One and Only;
> Allah, the Eternal, Absolute;
> He begetteth not, Nor is He begotten;
> And there is none like unto Him.

I learned this verse while also learning its meaning. The irony struck me immediately and seemed to me a dramatic signal of my new religious orientation. I had been a Christian, and this verse spelled out clearly the Islamic take on Christianity's vision of the Son of God. Monotheism, *tawhid* in Arabic, was very much the central idea of Islam and the driving force behind all of Ustadh Mahmoud's thinking.

When I visited Rufa'a, Mahmoud Mohamed Taha's hometown about a hundred miles south of Khartoum on the east bank of the Blue Nile, I often walked past the khalwa, the small retreat house where Ustadh Mahmoud spent two years in spiritual isolation after his imprisonment in the late 1940s. It was essentially a one-room building with a *rukuba* lean-to porch where one could enjoy a breeze from the giant river. The house was in the compound of his in-laws, and it was that family that cared for him during his period of reflection and isolation, a process known in Arabic as *khalwa,* which refers both to the act and place of retreat.

Rufa'a became my own retreat from the intense center of the Republican Brotherhood movement in Omdurman. In Rufa'a I could relax, enjoy family life, and ask my questions about the Republican ideology of people who had been living it for decades, in some cases, since the independence movement. And there were few dawn meetings, like there were at my house with the brothers in Omdurman. The members of the Rufa'a community of brothers and sisters were farmers, small shopkeepers, and primarily teachers in the many schools in the area, a region that had pioneered modern schooling during the colonial era. This community essentially adopted me, or claimed me, really, and helped me grasp the details of Ustadh Mahmoud's thinking over wonderful meals and talk and tea and river walks. In other words, I could see the Republican theory, the method I heard so much about in Omdurman, put into action in the daily lives of the brothers and sisters, my family, in Rufa'a. Ustadh Khalid El Haj, a long-time high school teacher and principal, and one of Ustadh Mahmoud's closest followers since the 1960s, became an important interpreter for me of the philosophy and its theology. He had authored a number of the Republican tracts and spoke authoritatively about Republican theology both patiently to me and as a public speaker to crowds, particularly at university sites in the capital. My "Rufa'a seminar" that deepened my understanding of Republican thinking came as a unified package in that it was delivered in the context of its practical application and in the town where that thinking was born. As everyone around me had a "village" of an ancestral nature to call home, I adopted Rufa'a as mine. In those early days, getting to Rufa'a was an adventure in itself, down the Medani road to Hassaheisa, and then a wait for the pontoon ferry across the Blue Nile.

Mahmoud Mohamed Taha's important book, *The Second Message of Islam* (1967; in Arabic, *a-risala a-thania min al-Islam*), was the product of the reflection he made during his khalwa retreat in Rufa'a in the late 1940s to early 1950s. The book is the centerpiece of Taha's unwavering constancy in thought and action; it was published in the midst of his own speaking tour across the country in the 1960s. Taha's point of view was that the debate on the future of Islam needed to be engaged; otherwise, the forces of extremism would be ceded all ground in the face of the Muslim world's general complacency. Ustadh Mahmoud's writings were the source both of his followers' understanding of Islam and their inspiration in the conduct of their lives. His writings led them to their fundamental insight that there was very little to value in Islam today if not for the modern approach proposed by their teacher. But Ustadh Mahmoud's writings were also an important source of the wider society's views of Mahmoud Mohamed Taha as everything from unbalanced Sufi sheikh to heretic to apostate, even *kaffir,* "unbeliever." Apparently Taha recognized this problem. He told an interviewer from an Arabic-language magazine, *Al-Awdaa a-Sudaniya,* "My approach is so new that I have become a stranger among my own people." Ustadh Mahmoud and his followers attempted to present their position within mainstream Islamic discourse and learned through verbal and physical abuse that ideological diversity was unwelcome in this arena in Sudan.

Violence never deterred the members of the Republican Brotherhood from their determination to demonstrate that Islam was the path to human freedom. They were shouted down in public and denounced from the pulpits of mosques by extremist ideologues and their representatives. They were beaten up while trying to give public lectures. At the same time they did have a strong consciousness of how the wider society was reacting to their message, and they spent time listening to those opposed to them. I remember during the days leading up to President Nimeiry's 1983 crackdown on the group, how the Republican leadership sent delegations of brothers out to mosques in the Khartoum area to listen to the Friday sermons, which had been containing more and more government-sanctioned invective against the Republicans. I participated in this investigation, but only in the protective way that the brothers organized my activities. My assignment was to go to Tuti Island's mosque to listen to the Friday sermon with one of the brothers who had family there. Tuti was a lovely garden spot in the middle of the Blue Nile, a cooling ten-minute ferryboat ride in those days from Khartoum (there is now a fancy bridge). We took a pleasant boat ride, attended Friday prayers at the relatively calm mosque in Tuti, enjoyed lunch and returned to Omdurman with the intelligence we had gathered. I think the brothers thought I deserved a little "island vacation" from the tension that was developing quickly as Nimeiry tried to crush any opposition to his planned implementation of sharia law in the country.

Many Islamic reformists of the moderate-liberal-progressive spectrum have captured the imagination—and hope—of the West by describing a "peaceful Islam" or emphasizing the etymological connections between the words for Islam and peace (*salaam*). The Islamic elephant in the room, so to speak, appears to be sharia law and how it fits into Islam's current and future practice. Mahmoud Mohamed Taha and his colleagues tackled this issue head on and it has always been the centerpiece of controversy about the Republican Brotherhood.

The debate over sharia is essentially one of how the Qur'an is to be operationalized. Islamic polemicists such as Sayid Qutb (1906–1966), the Egyptian Muslim Brotherhood stalwart who was a contemporary of Mahmoud Mohamed Taha, promoted what could be called a static approach to sharia, stressing that sharia must be observed as they believed it was described in the

Qur'an. Taha called his own approach "evolutionary," one that would move humankind to the level of Islam practiced by the Prophet Mohamed. Taha wrote in the introduction to the fourth edition of *The Second Message of Islam*,

> Muslims seem unaware of the need to evolve Shari'a.
> They continue to think that the problems of the twentieth
> century may be resolved by the same legislation that
> resolved the problems of the seventh century. This is
> obviously irrational. Muslims maintain that the Islamic
> Shari'a is perfect. This is true, but its perfection consists
> precisely in its ability to evolve, assimilate the capabilities
> of individuals and society, and guide such life up the ladder
> of continuous development.[1]

The texts of the Republican Brotherhood, the books written by Mahmoud Mohamed Taha and the books, tracts, and odes written by other members of the organization were critically important to my understanding of the social life of the Brotherhood. These works provided the philosophical backdrop for all Republican activities, from their meetings with Ustadh Mahmoud and each other, to public presentations of the movement's ideology, to the pleasure the brothers and sisters derived from singing the contemporary hymns created out of odes on Republican themes.

The Republican ideology stood opposed to the political Islam of Osama bin Laden or Sayid Qutb. The Republicans viewed the Islamist perspective as an opportunistic use of the Qur'an's message to seventh-century members of the Prophet's community in Medina, to further contemporary political aims. The "reforms" promoted by Islamists are to accept the parts of that seventh-century revelation deemed useful to political objectives today, such as the infliction of cruel punishments instead of addressing poverty or the subordination of women. Iran, Sudan, and some of the states of northern Nigeria have been selective in the aspects of sharia that these "Islamic states," have applied in their criminal codes, in effect, "revising Shari'a," or "cherry-picking" Islamic law, in the American idiom.

Mahmoud Mohamed Taha provided contrast to the Islamist perspective above in his own Qur'anic commentary, *The Second Message of Islam*. In it may be found an Islamic reform "how-to": an activist (many said "too activist") approach or methodology that acknowledges the historical process of Qur'anic revelation and provides direction to the message of God that Taha believed was meant for the modern world. Mahmoud Mohamed Taha did not seek accommodation between Islam and the latest in Western mores; he wrote that his reading of the Qur'an found democratic values and social equality in places of honor. "We are not concerned here with deprecating Western civilization or belittling it, but rather wish to study it scientifically and put it in its proper place. We wish to acknowledge its advantages and advocate its reform so that it evolves into a true civilization rather than remaining satisfied with its material progress."[2]

My education in the Republican Brotherhood ideology was largely oral and experiential. But my understanding was expanded by the books, pamphlets, and odes written by Ustadh Mahmoud and other senior leaders of the movement. Communicating the message of the Republican Brotherhood was a crucial element of the organization's planning. Proselytizing the message was not as important a goal as becoming more articulate about the message for one's own understanding of it. And this could be accomplished through the act of trying to recruit people to the Republican idea.

Ustadh Mahmoud's written words guided his followers' daily lives. Passages from his works were committed to memory and inscribed on large posters, which decorated homes and offices of the members, often next to the beautifully drawn Qur'anic verses often found in Muslim living spaces. Islam is, as

Daniel Martin Varisco wrote, an "eminently textualized faith,"[3] and the Republicans' interactions with texts prepared them for the struggles they faced in representing their movement in the wider society. The Republican Brotherhood grew out of Sudan's modern educational history, of which literacy was a hallmark. I attended an early morning meeting in Rufa'a, which has developed a custom of communal reading and discussion of Republican texts under the leadership of Rufa'a Republican leaders such as Ustadh Khalid El Haj. This particular session was a gathering immediately after the predawn *subuh* prayer, a time when many Muslims return to bed after praying, for a little sleep before work. The industrious Republican community developed the habit of using this early waking hour for discussion of the latest Republican book. In this case, the scene was a group of older Republican sisters, some of whom were not literate, reading or being read to from the recently published Republican tract, *Hatha Hou a-Sadiq al-Mahdi* (This is Sadiq al-Mahdi), a critique of the Umma Party leader's religiously cloaked political aspirations, as he sought the position of prime minister once again in the 1980s. The reading group would share their first tea of the day while one sister would read a few pages each day and lead the group in questions and discussion of the text. Older housewives who otherwise would not participate in the debates taking place at Ustadh Mahmoud's meetings in Omdurman had a chance to do so in this manner, extending spirituality to the notion of family literacy.

The Second Message of Islam was essentially required reading for Republicans; as its author stated in the introduction, it is "the basic text for the Republican cause." The book is Mahmoud Mohamed Taha's "extremely concise" (his words) treatise on how the Qur'an applies to human life at this modern stage of its history and how, as a divine document, *al-mudhaf*, it evolves to guide every stage of existence. The Islamic belief is that the Qur'an exists at a spiritual level; that it was not created. An additional enigmatic note from Taha in the fourth edition of his book was that, because of the book's brevity, "further explanation and elaboration will follow in good time, God willing."

In that *The Second Message of Islam* provoked controversy with both its title and its content, I should attempt to summarize the book here. "Message" is a terribly loaded term for Muslims because of the Prophet Mohamed's unique role as "Messenger," or really as "seal" or final prophet of Islam. Casual or quick inspection of Taha's use of the term "second message" could raise issues of heresy and often did for Taha and his followers. In lands like Sudan, where Sufism is the dominant expression of Islam the Prophet Mohamed is seen as the first Sufi. I often compared Sudanese reverence for the Prophet to devotion to the Blessed Virgin Mary among my Italian and Irish forebears. I remember an emotional meeting where one of the brothers described his visit to the tomb of the Prophet Mohamed in Medina, Saudi Arabia, which left most of his listeners in tears.

But Taha's use of the term "message" is actually well understood among erudite Muslims, who divide the Prophet's period of messengerhood into two phases. It is noted, even in English translations of the Qur'an, during which phase of his prophecy the particular verse or text of the Qur'an was revealed. The first phase took place in the Prophet's home town of Mecca, where he began to receive revelations of verses of the Qur'an from the Angel Gabriel in 610 CE. These revelations continued for thirteen years until the *hijira*, or migration of the Prophet and his first followers to Medina, to escape persecution for their new beliefs. The Prophet continued to receive revelations through the Angel Gabriel in Medina, and these revelations are thought to be characterized by a more strident or social regulatory tone than those revealed in Mecca.

It was easier to understand the sense that Mahmoud Mohamed Taha had of the "First Message" in the context of what he called the principal dictates of its times, in the Prophet's community of

Medina. The elements he uses to illustrate the First Message represent transitional stages to human freedom that were part of the historical record of that era. *Jihad,* slavery, capitalism, gender inequality, polygamy, divorce, veiling, and gender segregation were given in Taha's book as examples of principles from the Qur'anic verses revealed during the Medinan period of Mohamed's Prophecy, a time when *al-muh'minun* ("the believers") were not capable of "properly discharging the duty of freedom."[4] Five of the principles above (gender inequality, polygamy, divorce, veiling and gender segregation) restrict women in some manner, speaking to Taha's lifelong concern for the improvement of women's status in society, and were the themes that brought so many women followers to his movement. At the same time, these restrictions were from the Medinan phase of Muslim society, which had conferred some progress on humankind from the time prior to revelation of the Qur'an. For example, the First Message had improved the status of women relative to their pre-Islamic circumstances, or jihad had provided means to spread the faith in a hostile era. But social restrictions still existed at this Medinan transitional stage, requiring the enforcement procedures developed in sharia law. Slavery was another example of an existing Arabian institution in which improvement of the conditions of slaves was made by the dictates of the First Message. The Qur'an's First Message made provisions that moved those enslaved toward emancipation, but the ancient institution itself could not be extinguished, in Taha's phrase, "by a stroke of the pen."[5] The point was that the believers of the Medinan community did not have the capacity to "discharge properly the duties of their freedom, [so] they lost this freedom, the Prophet was appointed as their guardian until they came of age."[6] Sharia law was introduced during the Medinan period, which reflected "a descent in accordance with the circumstances of the time and limitations of human ability."[7]

Although the details of Taha's Islamic theology may appear arcane, they diverged deeply from mainstream orthodoxy, particularly on the issue of sharia. For his evolutionary stand on sharia, Ustadh Mahmoud was vilified by television preachers throughout the region as a "heretic"; he was subjected to the enmity of pulpits from Cairo to Khartoum, and twice put on politicized trials for related charges ending with his capital conviction for a concocted accusation of "apostasy" in 1985.

The 1985 trial was precipitated by the publication of a stern but respectfully worded leaflet by the Republican Brotherhood on December 25, 1984. Distributed by hand all over the Khartoum area and titled "Either This or the Flood" (see appendix), the document was a rallying cry for the repeal of the so-called "September laws." These laws were imposed with great fanfare by the regime of Sudan President Jaafar Nimiery in September 1983 and were essentially Nimeiry's version of "Islamic Law," that is, the new laws only partially followed conventional sharia. The announcement of the laws was marked by a great celebration that included the dumping of thousands of locally manufactured and imported bottles of beer and "sherry" into the Nile at Khartoum. These were tense times in Sudan. The war in the South had been rekindled by the government's imposition of these religious regulations even in Christian-dominated parts of the country, and the drumbeat leading up to the September 1983 laws had brought the Republicans out beginning in May 1983 to speak against the idea of the laws' imposition. About seventy of the Republicans including four of the sisters were arrested while engaged in their speaking platforms and thrown into jail. The Nimeiry regime had been under pressure from Islamist forces in Sudan, the Muslim Brotherhood led by Dr. Hassan al-Turabi in particular. From the regime's point of view, locking up the Republican brothers and sisters, despite their nonviolent protest, was a way to both appease those forces and make an example of a small group that posed little threat. The Muslim Brotherhood, bitterly opposed to Ustadh Mahmoud's ideas, represented the leading edge in Sudan of the conservative wave beginning to overtake the Muslim world.

The offending leaflet was a unique document, a flyer that summarized the Republican position against the imposition of sharia and the promotion of the revival of the Prophet's Sunna, and a plea to end the war in the South. The Republicans had long held that imposing sharia in a country with a significant non-Muslim minority (between 30 and 40 percent) would rip the nation apart. The leaflet blended Republican theology with a specific political agenda, an unusual stance for the usually nonpartisan Republicans. This led to the trumped-up treason charges resulting in Ustadh Mahmoud's arrest at the end of 1984. An operative paragraph of the leaflet read, "We call for the repeal of the September 1983 laws because they distort Islam, humiliate the People and jeopardize national unity." Mahmoud Mohamed Taha stood for the moral freedom represented by the verses of the Qur'an revealed to the Prophet in Mecca. By imposing a crude version of laws extending from the Medinan texts of the Qur'an, Taha felt strongly that Nimeiry's government was demeaning the hard-fought-for modernity of which Taha had been a champion since the struggle for Sudan's independence. The penultimate sentence of the pamphlet (see appendix) was "Religious fanaticism and backward religious ideology can achieve nothing for this People except religious upheaval and civil war." The war with the South in fact did not end until the signing of an uneasy peace agreement fifteen years later.

The Second Message of Islam was the curriculum that guided the Republican movement, an appropriate tool for a group of people with a high state of consciousness of their responsibilities as Muslims. In my "preliterate" state in Sudan my initial attraction to the movement was in what I could glean of its apparent Sufi heritage and what I learned through conversation and observation of its progressive position on a range of social issues.

I found it hard to distinguish where Sufism began and the hospitable Sudanese personality ended. Or to put it another way, were my new Sudanese friends so welcoming because of the heritage of Sufism in the Republican ideology? Among the Republicans there certainly was a strong effort to be *lateef,* a word that could be quickly translated as "nice" but which really refers to the range of behaviors around gentle, kind, friendly, graceful, mild. The Prophet was always thought to have been lateef, and lateef is an attribute of God. Lateef behavior was operationalized in the performance of tasks usually associated with what boys and young men were charged with doing around a household: serving guests and sharing space and resources, hauling dishes and so on back and forth between kitchen and eating place, for example. Women and girls were essentially assumed to be lateef as a matter of course.

But obviously the practice of Sufism has a deeper spiritual purpose, and the effort to be lateef indicated that one was consciously adjusting his behavior in order to travel the path of the Prophet Mohamed. Older men, even after they had acquired families and sons to do these many tasks for them, often continued with this behavior and were noted for it. According to Ustadh Mahmoud, the Prophet lived his life as a conscious role model for the rest of humankind for the rest of time.

The relationship between Sufism and the members of the Republican Brotherhood was a somewhat ambiguous one. One could say that Sufism was viewed as the movement's heritage but that its members had moved beyond that spiritual phenomenon. Sufism was the primary instrument of Islam's spread across Africa, so one could say fairly conclusively that all of the Republicans had Sufism in their families' past, if not their own practice of Islam. Ustadh Mahmoud himself and his generation were thoroughly steeped in it, particularly in the sense of the community atmosphere of almost obligatory membership in a Sufi *tariqa,* or sect. The sects themselves were founded by different Sufi teachers, and this was Sufism's structure: built on the relationship between a Sufi teacher and student. The particular Sufi path was passed from teacher to student, going back to great teacher-philosophers of the past, like Abdel Gadir al-Jailani of Baghdad, the eleventh-century founder of the Gadaria Sufi sect and related groups common in Sudan.

The contributions of Sufism to Republican thinking were deep and rich. But the Republicans were wary of contemporary Sufi organizations in that Sufis were often accused of practicing *shirik*. The Arabic root of the word *shirik* is related to that of the word for "partner," which leads to the definition of shirik as placing various idols as "partners" to God. Idolatry contradicts the fundamental monotheistic principle of Islam, that there is no God but God; God has no partners, no equals. And Sufis have been accused of the Islamic offense of shirik in their emphasis on ritual, the visitation of saints, and the close relationship between the Sufi sheikh and follower. Sufis and the Republicans would counter that they are not "worshipping" sheikhs or saints, but simply following closely in the path of those who served as role models of faith.

I liked to visit my good friend Hamad-a-nil in Abu Haraz, not too far from Rufa'a on the east bank of the Blue Nile. A considerable portion of this small town was given over to sprawling ancient cemeteries, which were dominated by the *qubbab,* tombs, of some of the founders of Sudan's Sufi sects. The founders commanded the best views in town from their tombs perched on the highest points of the cemetery. The domed architecture of these domed tombs was the heritage of Sudan's occupation by the Ottoman Turks in the late eighteenth and the nineteenth centuries. Today they are painted in pink, blue, yellow, and, of course, the Prophet's green in bright contrast to the surrounding dun color of the dusty savannah. The tombs attracted adherents of the particular sheikh, or simply people who collected all the wisdom of those who had gone before them. My friend knew the life story of each of these "saints," and the lore associated with his tariqa. My favorite saint, however, did not have a tomb over his burial site, just rubble of Blue Nile red bricks. On our visits

Hamad-a-nil would always quote a rhyming couplet associated with this sheikh, *"al ma indu biniya, ma be-du tahiya?"* ("Just because I don't have a tomb, you're not going to salute me?"), in a sense signaling the physical-spiritual connection visitors made with those buried in this vast place of rest. In an earlier day of the movement, Ustadh Mahmoud would also lead groups of brothers and sisters to the cemetery at Abu Haraz in appreciation of the Sufi knowledge of the past, and perhaps with a picnic lunch. One of the great pleasures inside the domed tombs was to listen to the Republican munshid, someone who could sing the hymns associated with the teachings of the particular holy man, with the sound reverberating off the tomb's dome and all around the cemetery. I tried this once on a visit to Karen, Eritrea, not far from the Sudan border, in the tomb of a saint related to the Mirghani family of the Khatmiya Sufi tariqa. I had given a talk at the University of Asmara the previous day and then traveled to Karen with my friend Ghirmai Negash. I asked him to come inside with me, but instead he waited outside while I paid my respects to the holy man. For some reason the atmosphere inspired me to sing the Khatmiya-related *qaseeda* (ode), "For the Sake of God, Ya Hassan!" which had been a very popular hymn among the Republicans. When I came out of the tomb Ghirmai thought that there had been a crowd with me inside, but it was just me and my echo.

Hamad-a-nil's exuberance in these visits to the saints of Abu Haraz extended to his crawling under the canopied grave site to take up a handful of cool sand, which he would pour on my bare feet. "Baraka," he would say as a blessing from the particular saint. The world of Islamic orthodoxy would frown on all of the behavior related to visits of the saints as shirik, in this sense charging that one was seeking intervention with God through the saints. But Hamad-a-nil and the Sufis would maintain that they knew very well how to approach God directly, and their investment in respect for the saints was simply appreciating the lives of their fellow Sudanese who had trod the path of the Prophet before them and appeared to have established closer connections to God. These were practices of warmth and intimacy shared among brothers.

A gnawing question for me was if Sufis had so much in common with the thought and practice of Ustadh Mahmoud and the Republicans, why were there not more Sufis joining Republican ranks? The explanation lies both in the historical Sudanese multigenerational attachment that those devoted Sufis had to their ancestral tariqa and in the educated consciousness that most often produced new recruits to the Republican ideology. Abandoning rote ritual for a deep critical discussion of faith was a difficult transition, but certainly not impossible as shown by the many Republicans who joined Ustadh Mahmoud directly from Sufi *turuug* (sects). The Republicans were highly conscious of the separation they had from the Sufi focus on ritual. They referred to the general Sufi approach—somewhat jocularly—as *dhikir bidun fikr,* or "remembering God without reflection," a performance of ritual that does not promote spiritual progress.

Mahmoud Mohamed Taha's quest was to the state of absolute individual freedom. *Tariq Mohamed,* the path of the Prophet, was a methodology well known to Sufi adherents. For Mahmoud's critics, the superficial Sufi-tariqa elements of his movement were easy targets—derisively referring to Mahmoud Mohamed Taha as "Sheikh Mahmoud," for example. This also meant that the potential Republican was required to look deeply into the movement's ideology and theology before making the commitment to join. But Mahmoud Mohamed Taha was of the school of thought that maintained that the Prophet was the original Sufi, and that the Prophet's approach, his *ibada,* was what would lead to human perfection. The Prophet's practice was the highest standard to which all humans should aspire. One could learn to follow the prayer of the Prophet with greater and greater concentration, the clearest manifestation of his practice, until more of the Qur'an's knowledge was revealed through this process of prayer. Ahmed Dali, who led the Republicans' public speaking campaigns in the 1970s and 1980s, recalled a Qur'anic verse that pointed to the daunting aspects of this task: "One cup of ink could be used to write the revealed portions of the Qur'an, but to write the hidden portions would require more ink than would fill the ocean."

In an important sense Mahmoud Mohamed Taha engaged in dialogue with classical Sufi practice. He studied the Qur'an deeply, and a tome by the eleventh-century Sufi master, al-Ghazzali, *Reviving Religious Studies,* was always an important reference for him. The book detailed the method of prayer. Sufi practice was clearly the source of Ustadh Mahmoud's deep understanding, but he was constantly aware of the need to find a way for Islam in the modern world, and Sufism, particularly in Sudan, represented something "folkloric" to him and many of his followers, and Sufism is always local in practice. "Today's Sufis have lost their way," a follower remembered Taha saying. Ustadh Mahmoud did not cite any *silsila* or chain of knowledge from sheikhs of the past to bolster his authority, common among Sufi leaders; he simply shared his interpretation and assisted his followers in understanding it as the Path of the Prophet. His critics would label this "esoteric knowledge," rarely seen and beyond most Muslims' understanding. Taha viewed knowledge as the product of appropriately intense prayer, available to all sincere travelers on the Path of the Prophet.

In traditional Sufi practice, one isolated oneself to attain this state of awareness, the khalwa notion mentioned above. Another Prophetic saying went, "Be in this world as a stranger, or as a passerby." But Ustadh Mahmoud's perspective was that the contemporary world could not afford to have its most spiritually aware people retreat from it. After his own intensive retreat at Rufa'a in 1948–51, Taha never again sought to exclude himself from his society. His followers learned from him that we must see improving the world we live in as part of a spiritual project. And the follow-up to this was that we cannot immerse ourselves in prayer if the broader sociocultural context is not in order, if there is no food on the table or the children are in need of care. If the conditions are right, then immersing yourself in prayer is a retreat from the world around you, momentarily. Achieving this *hudur*, intense concentration in prayer, was a difficult challenge in the modern world. But Ustadh Mahmoud stood as the role model for his followers. My friend Mohamed al-Fatih told me, "Ustadh Mahmoud's life was at the level of practice—100 percent—he was beyond theory. He lived the theory. While we followers were mostly at the level of theory. We could talk about it, yes, but were we living it?"

Although the great historical frame for Republican practice was Sufism, its contemporary grounding was in women's rights, human rights, social justice, and other elements of the progressive agenda. As Ustadh Mahmoud saw it, social progress and Sufism came together in *al-mu'amalat* (social transactions). He wrote in *The Second Message of Islam,* al-mu'amalat "regulate the relationship between one individual and another in the community."[8] These are good acts, the acts necessary to keep society moving and noble. Mohamed al-Fatih remembered the way Ustadh Mahmoud made this point at a group meeting, taking it to the plane of absolute individual freedom: "There are some things to be in a hurry about, other things not to hurry you. Prepare for *al-duniya* [this world] as if it would never end. Prepare for *al-akhira* [the next world] as if it will come tomorrow."

I had come to Sudan to learn, and what I found myself doing among my Republican brothers and sisters was learning how to learn. This interested me on so many levels. As a social scientist-in-training, I was drawn to the discussion and performance of methodology; all of this Sufi lore was really about methodology, the how-to of getting closer to God. As an American who had come to Sudan seeking immersion in the culture, I was repeatedly struck by the intense expertise around me, that everyone was working on becoming better human beings—and that they had found a path to do so. My daily exposure to poverty in Sudan, particularly in the sites of my dissertation research, made me think about how this poor African society could produce these advanced religious thinkers who seemed to have figured out how faith, family, and community could thrive in balance. And that everyone around me was most willing to tell me how to do it, too, drew me deeper into the community and made me look forward to the next lesson.

3
A Human Rights Culture

M y accepting the invitation to move into one of the houses of the Republican Brotherhood coincided with my learning that the cohesive and consistent body of thought taught by Mahmoud Mohamed Taha was applied every day in the lives of his followers. The most intensive laboratory for this application was the collection of "brothers' houses" scattered around the southern part of the Omdurman neighborhood of Thawra, and serving effectively as an experiment in democratic living. These houses were where the credo from Mahmoud Mohamed Taha's book *The Second Message of Islam*—reconciling the needs of the individual with those of the community—was made concrete on an experimental and daily basis. Men, some single, some married migrants to town, lived communally in these houses to be as close as possible for daily exposure to their teacher. There were brothers' houses in other towns as well, including Wad Medani, Atbara, and El Obeid. A small group of the sisters had a communal living arrangement in Ustadh Mahmoud's home. While Ustadh had told me at our first encounter that, unlike the conventional Sufi sects, the Republican Brotherhood did not have an initiation ritual for new members, I felt that my first Ramadan with the Republican brothers and sisters more than served that purpose. Ramadan, the holy month of fasting that is one of Islam's most fundamental practices, introduced me to a Republican life of discipline in a very physical way. My first Ramadan was also my initial exposure to the seriousness of every element of the Republican message. And Ramadan was a public stage on which the Republicans could demonstrate—in a context well known to all their neighbors and countrymen and women—that the Republican ideology provided the best blueprint for modern life.

I had been exposed to Ramadan's rigors as a high school teacher in neighboring Chad, where I had learned that it was mighty difficult to keep a class of adolescents focused on my lesson when half its members got up to spit out the window just about every minute. My Muslim Chadian students' understanding that swallowing saliva constituted breaking the fast was certainly not part of the Republican perspective on spit. But in that torrid Sudan June of my first Ramadan fast, saliva did not go far to make a day without food or water an easy obligation. As the temperatures in Sudan reached 100 degrees or more, I confess that I considered delaying my total embrace of the Republican way of life until after that first Ramadan was over. But after meeting Ustadh Mahmoud and many of the other brothers I was so drawn to the movement and moved by its hospitality that I jumped into my first Sudan Ramadan during Khartoum's most searing month. While the very young, frail, pregnant, and ill are exempted from the Ramadan fast, I realized that it would not have been possible for a healthy person like myself to avoid fasting in such close living quarters; Islam is an intensely social religion. God in His mercy had made Ramadan a movable obligation, a month in the lunar calendar so its dates moved up eleven days each year in the Western calendar. A cooler Ramadan in Sudan was years away at that point.

Ramadan was associated with fasting before the coming of Islam to Arabia. But the revelation of the Qur'an made Ramadan one of Islam's five *arkan*, or "pillars," that must be followed by observant Muslims, meaning complete abstinence from all food, drink, and sex from before the sun rose to sunset. I found poetry in the scriptural test of when the day begins: when the dawning light allows one to distinguish a white thread from a black one. Like prayer, another one of the pillars, fasting has the dual nature of individual practice combined with the aggregate of community participation, an equation that can give the believer enormous satisfaction. In other words, I eventually learned that it is difficult to sustain either prayer or the fast by oneself, particularly as I moved back to my life in the secular United States. The Sufis who sought refuge for prayer and fasting in isolated spots in rural Sudan believed that they were earning extra baraka for this feat of deprivation.

The sacrifices required of the Muslim during Ramadan were tests of the limits of human physical endurance. If we were waiting for God to come, what better way to prepare? There were many Republican exercises that prepared and expanded the mind for its contests—the lectures, the readings, the discussions among themselves and with men and women on the streets. But the test provided by Ramadan, particularly when it fell in Sudan's heat, was all about the most basic of human needs: nourishment and water. Belief in Islam is thought of as faith, an exercise of the spirit. But Ramadan shows us how Islam is also about how physical endurance is the essence of humanness. This issue works into Ustadh Mahmoud's progressive consideration of Islam as well, that Islam evolves with human beings' understanding of it themselves. With intense prayer, intimate knowledge of God increases, until the desire for food and other animalistic aspects of our nature fade away.

But my test in the heat was in the here and now, and was not to be joined alone. And when there are young men involved, there will be a competitive element. Perhaps not as crude as the Ramadan spitting contests of my Chadian students, but

A Human Rights Culture

certainly one that stimulates our endurance. My residence, the *beyt-al-akhwan,* the "brothers' house" resonated with the question all through Ramadan: *Saim wala fatir? saim wala fatir?* (Are you fasting today or not?). And conversation among the brothers often moved toward how many days one has fasted *this* Ramadan versus how successful one had been the previous year. Improving on one's performance of faith was another Republican hallmark.

Of course, I stumbled myself a number of times in my own pursuit of Ramadan perfection. I remember that my first trip to visit brothers in Wad Medani took place during Ramadan. In Wad Medani I stayed as a guest in the home of Medani's Republican leader, Ustadh Saeed. There was less commotion in that family home in the morning—no early communal prayer or meeting— so I slept through the morning's call to prayer. The first thing I did after waking was to take my antimalaria medication (a precaution eventually abandoned as I gained more baraka). A brother in the room saw me swallow the little pill and asked, "So Steve, you're not fasting today?" I replied that of course I was. And he quickly provided the new information that taking medicine broke the fast, God's point being that one takes medicine if one is sick. And the sick were excused from fasting. I did observe the fast the rest of the day out of solidarity, but was disappointed to have my record spoiled so early in the fasting month.

The spare cuisine that accompanied the sunset breaking of the fast for the brothers from the houses in Ustadh Mahmoud's neighborhood suited the Republican/Spartan design of the whole month. Plenty of baraka for everyone. That June, my first attempt at fasting, was also the time of school holidays, which meant that Republican schoolteachers from outside of Khartoum: the Gezira, Kordofan, maybe from the East or the North, came to spend the holidays near their teacher, which meant that they would lodge with us in the already cramped brothers' houses. As the hour of sunset approached, the brothers would ready themselves for the evening by bathing and dressing, activities that often followed a late afternoon nap. Then, from each of the four houses a procession (*masira*) of brothers would march—chanting the name of God—through the neighborhoods to the home of Ustadh Mahmoud. They would form a half circle in front of the house, joined by the sisters who grouped to one side, and thirsty, hungry, and hot they would continue the chant for the forty-five minutes to one hour before the sunset azan signaling the end of the day's fast. Brothers and sisters who lived outside of the network of "brothers' houses" would also start to arrive and join the *dhikir*. The standard expectation of practicing Muslims during Ramadan was that the fast should not be an excuse for lightening one's daily load of work, but I did find this late-in-the-day dhikir an additional test of membership in this intense community of believers. The heat and my intensely dry mouth would sometimes force my willing spirit to just sway with the chant with my mouth closed. It was perhaps a test—within the limits of the fasting day—of our potential to forget about food and just focus on God. It was a practice for the time that Republicans were waiting to come.

But not yet. This world was still hot, and many hungry people had just chanted to bring the sun down. So labor was divided and tasks shared to get ready for the meal. Some of the brothers would bring the long straw mats out from Ustadh Mahmoud's house and lay them in rows ready for prayer in the empty lot just west of the house. Other brothers would bring out the heavy aluminum pans filled with a large mound of *asida* (sorghum or millet porridge) and many spoons. The dozen or so pans were placed here and there on the mats, and brothers crouched around them, perhaps eight to ten to a pan. The tin pan descended from the ancient *gada* wooden bowl, still used by many good Sufi communities around the country for their communal meals. Then, a third group of brothers would come out of Ustadh Mahmoud's kitchen—where the sisters had been fasting and cooking—with large pails of *mulah,* a meatless okra-based sauce to be poured over the porridge. Everyone would then dig into the porridge with the spoons provided, while some of the brothers would go around with the sauce pail to try to replenish the dish until there was no more. Off to the side brothers could help themselves to lemonade or *karkedeh,* the popular Ramadan drink made from dried hibiscus petals that had been prepared in large plastic barrels to quench the brothers' thirst. If a particularly large crowd came for this simple meal (everyone was welcome, so the numbers were not necessarily predictable), a garden hose would find its way into the barrel in order to serve more guests. Loaves and fishes, Sudan style.

I found this sunset scene at once warm and overwhelming. In order to eat from the pan I had associated with what we were using in the brothers' house to wash clothes by hand, I had to squeeze into the circle of brothers gathered tightly around it, all crouched on one knee, and balance like that while stabbing at the wobbly porridge mass in the pan—if I had been lucky enough to find a spoon! Those with more fortitude than I (or longer arms) could eat this steaming hot concoction with a bare right hand. I admired those who saved space around the circle by looping their free left arm over the shoulder of the next brother. In my weakened state—new to fasting and to the heat—I often was able to get only a spoonful or two before the dish was gone. The multitasking required—crouching and balancing while scooping asida—was beyond my skill set at that point. I did receive a great deal of encouragement from around the pan, but the brothers were hungry, too.

Next the mats were cleared, and the men lined up for the sunset prayer. In those days at the height of the movement and with the teachers from the provinces in town, there could be two hundred people for the meal and prayer. At the conclusion of the prayer that first Ramadan, while it was not yet dark, I would sometimes be so exhausted that I would just go home and go to bed and sleep through the late night supper or predawn *sahur* without eating anything else for the next twenty-three hours. I was determined to participate in this most binding of rituals.

This simple, crowded, ascetic Ramadan *fatur* (breakfast) was hardly the norm in Sudan, a culture with a great love of delicious food—and Ramadan was its showcase. I sometimes snuck away to the homes of friends, both Republicans with families nearby and non-Republicans, to see how everyone else feted Ramadan, which also helped me to better understand the point of the simple meal at the home of Ustadh Mahmoud. My agenda was also to simply fill my gut for the long fasting haul. El Tayib Hassan, another Republican storyteller, told me that once he was at the university on a Ramadan day, and although he had been invited to fatur at the home of a friend, raced in a taxi before sunset to the home of Ustadh Mahmoud in order to share the meal with the brothers. He arrived as the men and boys gathered around the pans, and he invited his taxi driver to get out of the car and join them. The driver parked his car, got out, took one look at the minimalist meal being served, shouted "Thanks!" and jumped back into his taxi to speed off toward home and presumably a heartier meal. It was a challenge to recruit Sudanese to this way of life. But the point is that the Republicans conducted their Ramadan rituals—the procession, the dhikir, the meal, and the prayer—out in the open where anyone passing by could observe an extraordinary community applying their philosophy in a consistent manner. Everyone was clearly enjoying each other's company, but this was also an invitation for passersby to stop, look, and listen to a group of Muslim men and women who were emphasizing the spiritual elements of the holy month.

An experience in a wintry Cairo ten years later expanded my horizon on the Ramadan theme of hospitality as an extension of simple spirituality. I had spent an entire Ramadan day in Cairo with a terribly darwish Sudanese guy, who had once been an active Republican brother. We visited more than a dozen of the many tombs scattered across Cairo of holy men and women of the family of the Prophet. As the day moved toward sunset, I started to complain to my friend that I had no idea where we would break the fast ourselves. The streets of Cairo were clearing out as even the taxi drivers drove home to their own meals. He essentially told me not to worry so much about this, that we would eat. We arrived at the mosque of Sayda Zainab in one of Cairo's popular quarters, the tomb of the revered granddaughter of the Prophet Mohamed. At that hour there were few people there save the poor, and my friend told me to wait there while he went to hunt for some food for us. I settled down on the ground with my back up against the wall of the tomb, and enjoyed the call to sunset prayer echoing from mosques all over the city. As soon as the call was completed, men and women shuffled over to me and placed small dishes of delicious breakfast foods, beans decorated with eggs, cheese, tomato, crunchy falafel, and lots of loaves of bread. The Egyptians saw this stranger in their midst who apparently had no place to go, sitting outside an important mosque at the breaking of the fast. They shared their meals with me, and it may have been the most delicious food I had ever eaten.

More than forty-five minutes after the call to sunset prayer my darwish friend returned bearing a small bare bowl of simmered beans without the standard relishes of sesame oil, or anything that accompanied the dishes of my Sayda Zainab friends almost an hour earlier. But I enjoyed it with him while telling him of what to do the next time he found himself at this mosque not knowing where his next meal was coming from.

At the conclusion of Ramadan, when most of the visiting brothers returned home to their schools, towns, and villages, we went back to the routine life of the brothers' houses, lucky to have daily access to Ustadh Mahmoud. The residential geography of the movement provided powerful clues as to the relationships between Mahmoud Mohamed Taha and his followers. Ustadh Mahmoud lived in an old house made of the mud-clay material, jalous, common to the region's architecture. The brothers' houses, each housing fifteen to twenty single male members of the movement, were all within a fifteen-minute walk to the home of Ustadh Mahmoud. In a mixed working-class/middle-class suburb of Khartoum, the houses were essentially single-family dwellings, which had been rented by individual brothers on behalf of a group. The institution of the brothers' house, beyt-al-akhwan, went back to the earliest days of the movement, and in fact had been a feature of Mahmoud Mohamed Taha's political party in the 1940s. In the past, brothers who were traveling around the country to spread the movement's message would seek shelter with local Sufis. Many of the married members of the movement also made their homes in the Thawra district north of Omdurman, to be near Ustadh Mahmoud. It was common to graduate from the bachelors' quarters of the brothers' houses to marry and start a family within a few blocks of the two sites.

The invitation to move into one of the brothers' houses was exactly what I had been looking for in Sudan: my quest to climb inside the Sufi experience was complete. I brought my suitcase from the apartment I had been using in Khartoum and shoved it under one of the many beds in the house, thinking I had now claimed my own space in a Sufi *zowiya* (a place of Sufi lodging). What had in fact happened was that the brotherhood's claim on me had become much stronger as I presented myself willingly to a new way to see the world, not to mention the claim that any brother in the house had to borrow a belt or a shirt hanging out of my suitcase. As I look back on this communal living experience I think about how quickly I adjusted to the crowd—not minding stepping on or over an enormous pile of shoes and sandals left at the door to a room, and then searching for my shoes afterward. Privacy is exchanged for a deeply fraternal solidarity.

I may have felt very special in my new residence, but I had in fact followed a familiar path to being recruited by the

A Human Rights Culture

Republican Brotherhood. Men and women joined the movement after conversations with friends and after attending Republican events such as weddings or smaller meetings. At least a third of the members were family members of Republicans or married into the organization. Not every Republican took up residence in one of the brothers' houses; for example, a man already married who became Republican would not have much reason to live in one of these residences. Some of those living in the brothers' houses had left families that seriously disapproved of Ustadh Mahmoud and his message of change. But the casual and fluid nature of the houses did mean that they usually consisted of a core population of around twenty brothers with plenty of room for those who needed a place to stay for the night or a week or longer. Brothers based in other towns of Sudan would often adopt one of the Omdurman houses as the place they always stayed when coming to see Ustadh Mahmoud and/or to commune with the brotherhood. This was a most common practice by Republican teachers from the rural regions who stayed in Omdurman for the school holidays.

A crowded house with limited sleeping spaces had its own system of organizing the human flow. Beds being in many cases just about the only item of furniture in a Sudanese house, they served all day long as places to sit, nap, read, eat, have a conversation, in addition to sleeping. These were invariably single beds, either made of metal or the traditional angareb of wood and sisal webbing, so they could easily be moved around—in or outside depending on the heat. The brothers' houses were constructed as one-family homes for the most part, so they only had maybe two "bedrooms" and a large "saloon" or living space (from the Arabic for "salon"), and a *berenda* (veranda) or two. And all houses in this area were surrounded by a walled housh, or courtyard, where one could sleep in the hot weather and/or have cooking space. Many houses also had a palm tree or two for shade in corners of the housh.

The brothers' house was not simply a place to crash. This was an institution that served as the crucible for the movement, where its leadership was trained and its disciples formed into a cadre to serve the membership and each other. While the Republicans styled their residence *beyt-al-akhwan*, or "brothers' house," the phenomenon was a common one across Africa. I had first come across the concept in a well-known 1967 monograph by the anthropologist Leonard Plotnicov, *Strangers to the City: Urban Man in Jos, Nigeria.* In fact, I had used the book in the doctoral qualifying exams I had taken not long before leaving for Sudan from the sociology department at Michigan State University. Plotnicov describes the urban living of the men who left homes and families in rural areas and came to town in search of work, and shared "bachelors' quarters" in order to save money. In urban Sudan, where *beyt azaba* was the local term for this arrangement, such houses had an unsavory reputation for attracting loose women and alcohol—not something a neighborhood of respectable families would embrace.

The brothers were, of course, aware of this image problem and made every effort to be good and discreet neighbors and not let disgrace descend on the neighborhood. I remember one morning walking out of our house and in front of a house just two doors down, with my Sudanese research assistant, Shams. A woman came out of the house and shouted at Shams, not knowing that I could understand her and that I was in fact, a neighbor—that Shams should not let that "foreigner see the shameful, dirty condition of our street!"

Maintaining the cleanliness, decorum, and above all, the spirituality of the house was the responsibility of the sheikh, the head brother in the house appointed by Ustadh Mahmoud. The use of the term "sheikh" in this context was an expression of the Sudanese sense of humor, light commentary on the old Sufi orders which were all headed by a sheikh. In fact in order to dim the luster on that title a bit more, everyone in the house was called sheikh; there was even a Sheikh Steve in their midst. But the act of leadership itself was taken very seriously; if the house functioned in an orderly manner, the brothers would be able to immerse themselves in prayer—the most important activity in the house and the reason for its existence. Everywhere you looked in the house you could find prayer rugs, *"mislaya,"* of every description, made from straw matting, woven in a Chinese mill, or made from a discarded sugar sack.

I was talking to a sister, Selwa Ahmed El Bedawi, about the simplicity of life in these houses, and she recounted how Ustadh Mahmoud communicated the imperative of simplicity as a natural phenomenon. Taha had been on a speaking tour near the western town of El Obeid where drought was a perennial problem, and he climbed a hill with a group of brothers. He pulled up a small sapling and took it around and asked the brothers to smell it. "It smells intelligent!" said Ustadh Mahmoud. "It smells intelligent because it thrives here taking only what it needs. It takes the moisture that it needs and no more." This was the kind of simple efficiency with which we should lead our lives, he said, modeled for the movement in the brothers' houses and in his own.

Ahmed Dali was a house leader for many years and worked hard to maintain a stimulating atmosphere for the brothers in the house. He did a doctorate with me at Ohio University during his years of exile following Ustadh Mahmoud's execution. Dali was also the principal voice of the Brotherhood in Khartoum's streets and squares at the height of the movement. He and I talked a great deal over the years about the role of the house sheikh and about the concept of leadership in the movement. He told me, in that the brothers in the house were people who had made a choice to follow Ustadh Mahmoud and not the traditional Islamic conventions of Sudan, they were a group who knew what they wanted and had strong views on leadership. Many of them were fed up with the staid wider society and its ways that didn't seem to be going anywhere. They wanted leaders who acted themselves as they told others to act, which was not the norm among Sudan's political class. Remaining close to his followers was also an important element of Ustadh Mahmoud's leadership. I remember Taha's charge to a group of brothers departing in a predawn hour on a mission to spread the Republican Brotherhood message in southern Sudan. "You should sit on the ground when you talk to them," he recommended, continuing on about trying to reach people at their level to persuade them of your good ideas, instead of talking down to them.

Dali also made the point about the leader of the house also serving as the imam for the household's observance of the early morning prayer—and for any other time that the group prayed together. "You can't lead them in prayer if you can't lead them in every other example, like keeping the house clean," Dali told me. Clean house, clean hearts. This notion stuck with me in an important way; that a person praying in a group needed to have confidence in the intentions and morals of the prayer leader in order to feel that his or her own prayers were acceptable to God. What I was learning from my Republican Brothers was that this link between individuals in prayer also applied to the social and political processes of life—that this kind of confidence in your spouse, your teacher, your boss, or your president, for example, secured your confidence in the product of all your interactions together. Again, I was impressed with the pressure on one another for high standards of behavior that everyone accepted as members of the group, but it also helped me understand why the organization was so small.

Keeping busy, keeping occupied in the mission of the movement, "remembering God a lot"; these were the primary tasks at hand for the brothers in the house. Although some of the brothers had come from lives where they had been observant Muslims, for others the Republican experience was a transformation, and everyone was ready to tell the tale of how they came to take up the path of the Prophet. One brother who had had a reputation as a carouser happened to hear Ustadh Mahmoud speak in his hometown at an early stage of his life and became a follower. Friends of the man's father, fellow merchants, heard about the son's new path in Islam and came to complain to the father about his decision to follow Ustadh Mahmoud and his controversial interpretation of Islam. The father told them, "Where were you when my son was misbehaving?? Go home and get *your* sons to follow Mahmoud Mohamed Taha!!"

It always seemed to me that the intense 24/7 activity of the brotherhood, particularly as it was centered in the brothers' houses, was designed to keep Ustadh Mahmoud's followers on the path of the Prophet, and everyone was charged with looking out for each other to remain on that path. If you had any weaknesses or were distracted, all you had to do was follow the group's intense daily schedule, until you felt ready to step into more leadership roles yourself. In the preceding chapter I mentioned how I had approached Ustadh Mahmoud about "needing my space." Eventually I managed to find a way to do "my own thing" while enjoying and learning from everyone's company.

The group, *al-jama,* was certainly the collective mode in which much was done. Life in the brothers' house began before dawn with one of the brothers calling the *adhan* to waken and summon everyone for the day's first prayer. People stumbled out of sleep to make *wudu,* ablutions, using the ubiquitous plastic *ibreeks* scattered everywhere in the house. These containers were used to perform the ritual washing before prayer, with many of the brothers carefully facing the *qibla,* the direction of prayer (in this case, due east from Omdurman to Mecca) as they splashed cold water, washing hands, rinsing the mouth, nose, eyes, ears, head, arms up to the elbows, and then one foot after the other. Some took their time with this task, using it as an opportunity for further prayer—or reflecting on what one had done or where one had been with the eyes, mouth, feet, and so on as Ustadh Mahmoud recommended. Others were expeditious in their predawn ablutions, or just shocked by the cold water in the cooler months. Wudu could also be very refreshing in the hot months. I always admired the old men I saw thoroughly reaching a state of wudu with an ability to wash one foot while balancing on the other, an agile feat that I never mastered. When the weather was cold, and in that most people wore sandals all the time, the cold water of wudu could also be painful on the dry, chapped foot that could bear open sores on the heel. Many would ease the chapped heel with some sort of ointment.

Most of the brothers in the house were in fact getting up early to pray after not a particularly long night's sleep. An important aspect of the practice of the Republican Brotherhood's perspective on Islam was the "night prayer." This was, as Ustadh Mahmoud taught, the prayer of the Prophet's personal practice, or Sunna. And because it was important to the manner in which the Prophet practiced Islam, it was what Ustadh Mahmoud thought was a prayer that needed to be revived. He taught that the prayer be included in the daily obligations in order for Muslims to grow more like the Prophet Mohamed and become closer to God. The night prayer (called by the Republicans *giyam a-leyl*—"standing in the night"), was in effect a sixth prayer of the day and well known in Sufi practice. It was a completely independent prayer in that it was always prayed alone and was not introduced by the public call to prayer. The Prophet was said to have risen in the "last third of the night" (around 2–3 a.m. in Republican practice), and prayed many more *rukkat,* the pieces of prayer, than took place during the rest of the day's five other obligatory prayers. It could last forty-five minutes to an hour. Some were completely devoted to this practice; some did it occasionally; many who missed it would make up for it following prayers in the morning. I tried it and found it exhilarating— sometimes—particularly if I had been sleeping outside under the brilliant stars and was reasonably well rested. Otherwise, I'm afraid my excuse was the classic busy-American "I have to work

73

in the morning." But I admired those who were able to perform this duty, and often watched them from the fog of sleep as they prayed all night around me. Senior brothers and sisters might ask of those learning the ropes of the Republican way of practicing Islam: "Are you getting up for the night prayer?" or "I saw you practicing the night prayer last night," offered in support of the developing Republican and assessing one's progress toward success in the movement.

The night prayer was the signature of the movement, and prayer in general was an important topic of conversation among the brothers and sisters. The Republican criticism lobbed gently at their fellow Muslims was that "ordinary" Muslims were just going through the motions, literally, of prayer—performing their prayers as a religious duty. While it was a duty, of course, for the Republicans, Ustadh Mahmoud taught them that each time they pray their prayer should "improve" or move one in a progressive manner in one's relationship with God. I was told that the person at prayer should *housh juwa*, get "inside" prayer, to make it very successful. Each word of prayer, and prayers consist of verses from the Qur'an, should be an opportunity to reflect on its meaning—to try to get to the deeper meaning. I remember once dutifully saying my prayers in the brothers' house with a friend within earshot. When I was finished he teased me with "I don't think God said it quite like that," commenting on my less-than-perfect Arabic pronunciation. I'm sure I chuckled, but the comment also prompted me to work harder on my Arabic—a very Republican outcome.

The brothers' house prayer hall for the first group prayer of the day—the predawn *salat-a-subuh*—was the saloon, where there might still be some brothers sleeping as the prayer session got underway. Some of those sleeping might be given a paternalistic shake to get up and pray. Sleeping guests, though, would just be allowed to sleep through the prayer. Brothers would form lines behind the house sheikh as imam, some still wrapped in a sheet or a shawl if it was cold, and the prayer was completed in a few minutes. After the prayer the brothers would sit where they had ended the prayer and begin a meeting, led by the sheikh. The meeting was invariably opened by a group reading of the 97th chapter of the Qur'an, *Qadr*, the millenarian message of which had become the Republican anthem. Some of the brothers would be dozing while leaning next to someone or a wall, others would participate in the discussion in an animated fashion. A team of brothers would go out to the kitchen area and prepare a large kettle of tea with milk and plenty of sugar. One of the brothers, usually a younger member of the household—like in Sudan family situations—would pass a tray filled with glasses of this milky tea around the room and brothers would slurp—cooling the tea as they did so—and continue to listen to the discussion.

These early morning meetings were important to the wider brotherhood because it was one of the important places where the debates that fueled the direction of the organization began. Debate on Sudan's politics and the implications for the Republican outlook were common, along with explanations of the finer details of Ustadh Mahmoud's theology. Discussion of one of the organization's latest books or tracts might be on the agenda as well or plans for a larger Republican event or get-together. This also might be an occasion to listen to a qaseeda, a spiritual poem put to song, which could be sourced in Ustadh Mahmoud's theology or from a familiar old Sufi verse. For many of the brothers this was their introduction to debate in a democratic society. They had all come from communities and households where top-down, authoritarian or paternalistic approaches were how life was organized, and something different was in progress here. While these early morning meetings were preparatory discussions for the bigger meetings to be held at the home of Ustadh Mahmoud in the evenings, they were also where one learned to cooperate, to listen to opposing points of view, to make a contribution to a debate.

Setting a tone for the day, developing community spirit—this is what emerged from the early morning meeting, *al-jelsa sabahiya*, the first of the day's Republican encounters. From this meeting the brothers would get ready for the day of work or school. Brothers on the food team would divide up shopping responsibilities and plan the menu for the after-work lunch. Most of the brothers in the house would leave early to participate in their reason for living in the brothers' house: easy access to Ustadh Mahmoud. Every day Ustadh would greet his followers in the saloon of his house, where tea was also served in small glasses poured from a giant teapot. When a glass was drained, it was quickly refilled and handed to the next brother or sister. No germs would pass between brothers.

Brothers and sisters would cram themselves into the room in Ustadh's house, which had three or four beds against the wall and a few chairs near the door. Ustadh Mahmoud sat on one of these chairs; his wife, Amna Lotfi, would sometimes be seated next to him. They had been married for fifty-some years at that point, and Amna, referred to by all as "Umna Amna" (our mother, Amna) was younger than her husband. From her chair next to Ustadh Mahmoud at virtually all of the group's meetings, she represented the idea that women could fully participate in a Muslim movement. Years later, following her husband's execution, she helped to sustain the community with her warm presence.

Brothers and sisters would file in, greet Ustadh and his wife with handshakes and then find a seat on one of the beds or on the floor. Generally speaking women would take seats on the beds and the men would crouch on the mats on the floor. The agenda for this meeting would hardly vary—its purpose was to give the day a spiritual lift with a few of the spiritual poems sung and Ustadh occasionally interrupting the piece with questions on the spiritual meaning of this or that phrase. Learning was taking place in an atmosphere where everyone was much keyed into the context and to the teacher.

After an hour or so, people would leave for work or school from this meeting, perhaps humming the last hymn that had been performed. Some would drive off in cars to offices in Khartoum or elsewhere; others would look for transport on the main road or walk to their destinations. Some would remain at Ustadh Mahmoud's side either because they wanted to talk to him, they were to help with a project of some sort in the house, or just because being near him was the most joyous part of their day. I remember that I lingered behind once in order to share an observation with Ustadh Mahmoud from a novel I had been reading, an act that some in my house might criticize as "leisure." While my Republican brothers often pointed out to me how unique and revolutionary was the Republican ideology, I also found things in Sudan's everyday that struck me as related to or a source of Republican perspectives. I was reading E. M. Forster's *A Passage to India,* and found the exchange between Dr. Aziz and Cyril Fielding to have sparks of the Republican ideology in it. Mr. Fielding is astonished when Aziz shows him a picture of his late wife, who had been in purdah, as was common among Muslim Indians of the time. Fielding asks Aziz why the latter had shown him this picture, something the Englishman Fielding had assumed was forbidden in that he was not related to the wife. Dr. Aziz says that all men are his brothers, and when all men act like brothers, we will no longer have a need for purdah.

Although I did not feel that Ustadh Mahmoud was particularly impressed by my attempt to point out something in popular culture that I had thought was similar to Republican thinking, looking for such similarities was probably a sociologist's occupational hazard and helped me develop my vocabulary. Perhaps he found my sharing a novel of colonial India—with someone who was a veteran of Sudan's anticolonial struggle—ironic. It also reflected my grappling with trying to understand the complex theology I was hearing about every day and its implications for contemporary Sudan society. I was also trying to apply the theology to situations with which I was more familiar. My point in telling this story is to illustrate the remarkable accessibility that Ustadh Mahmoud provided to his followers and my own remarkable naivety in using it to see if the teacher approved of what I had learned. This incident had been something of a trial for me in that I was a bit intimidated by Ustadh Mahmoud's aura, or how it was portrayed by the brothers around me. I wanted to approach him only with perfect Arabic and with very wise observations. But I was also an apprentice student of Africa, and I found myself in awe of his modern ideas and wanted to get closer to the source. My concerns were probably oversensitive in that Ustadh, a very hospitable teacher, did spend quite a bit of time receiving darawish or simple Sufis from the country-side, who had their own ways of communicating with him. He also would see anyone who had any sort of problem, financial, medical, emotional, marital, and listen with great patience. He knew his followers very well and would often call on a brother or sister with some kind of capacity to help with these inquiries. The other Republican leaders were also very generous in assisting brothers or sisters in need.

In those days Sudan government offices would close around 2:00 p.m., and brothers would begin the trek home to a siesta and lunch, the biggest meal of the day. While some in the brothers' house would nap, a team would be busy preparing the afternoon meal. The brothers' houses and Ustadh Mahmoud were all strictly vegetarian, although meat played a big role in the cuisine of the wider society, and all the brothers came from that culture. But the Republican ideology was that everything was about peace, and the slaughtering of animals for their meat was considered by Ustadh Mahmoud to be an act of violence against the natural world. I remember once sitting in the saloon of Ustadh Mahmoud when a brother slapped a mosquito dead on his arm. "Why did you do that?" Ustadh Mahmoud asked him. When the brother responded that it had bit him, Ustadh

78

said, "You killed it for that?" The meat consumption issue was also connected to the social philosophy of the movement, which emphasized sharing of resources and solidarity with the poor (who could not afford to eat meat).

The cuisine was strictly vegetarian from the brothers' kitchens, and they would not let good food go to waste. During the Eid al Dahia celebrations, the major Muslim feast commemorating Abraham's willingness to sacrifice his son, Ismail, it is customary for every family to slaughter a sheep, as Abraham did, often in front of their houses. Our generous next-door neighbors had plenty of delicious *marara* to share and passed a big plate over the shared wall of our two compounds. Marara is the dish of organ meat from the sheep, a great holiday delicacy. The forbidden meat was consumed with laughter and gusto by the brothers in minutes. I also remember the sense of humor in the community when we would go out for delicious grilled fish in one of the shops next to the Nile. The fish was referred to by the brothers enjoying it as *nabaat a-bahar* ("a plant of the River").

When lunch was ready, we would gather in the main room of the house, where we had begun the day in prayer, and sit on the floor to eat together from two or three large bowls. Lunch might be a stew of eggplant, tomatoes, green pepper ,and red onion, served with the Sudanese flat bread made from sorghum, kisra. There might be a salad of *jirjir* (watercress), and watermelon, bananas, or another fruit for dessert. A subtle message conveyed in this process was the importance of men in Sudan learning how to cook—not generally something boys were exposed to in their mothers' kitchens. But with many of their prospective wives—the Republican Sisters—already in or getting ready to join Sudan's labor force, equality in household chores was an important value. Of course, as with everything, there was a gentle, joking competition between the four brothers' houses as to which one had achieved the higher level in life's two most basic arenas: food and religion (*din,* in Arabic). As the brothers in my house described our house situation, it had good din and good food. Comparatively speaking, in their view, the other three houses had: (a) good din and no food; (b) no din and good food; and (c) no din and no food. These ratings were of course not discussed with Ustadh Mahmoud or the senior leadership of the organization; they were used to poke fun at each other and intensify the great solidarity felt by members of each household.

When lunch was finished and the dishes cleaned and put away, brothers would nap or go off on their errands or get ready for the evening's activities. On rare occasions, there might be a chance to borrow a friend's TV and VCR and watch a video with appropriate content such as *Ghandi*. If it was Thursday or Friday, the Sudan weekend, the brothers from the four houses would have a procession to the home of Ustadh Mahmoud for the weekly dhikir before the sunset prayer. After the prayer on most weeknights, many brothers and sisters would go in teams or individually into town and sell the Republican books person-to-person on the street. The books were small self-published tracts that were written by members of the senior leadership of the brotherhood and described Republican thinking on a variety of issues, including the role of sharia law, the position of women in society, the "problem of Southern Sudan," and so on. Reports on book sales and public impressions of the Republican approach on the streets would then become an important agenda item for the evening's meeting with Ustadh Mahmoud.

When the brothers and sisters returned from *hamla* (campaign) on the streets, a meeting would be held every evening in the empty lot next to the home of Mahmoud Mohamed Taha. No one had a house big enough to hold this group, and the openness of the meeting in an open lot showed the wider society that the Republicans were not hiding or plotting anything, despite the Sudan government's implications and charges that they were. Beds and chairs were brought out from Ustadh's house for the sisters to sit on as well as members of the senior leadership.

And in the middle were the rows of mats, also used for prayer, where the brothers crowded together. Some, like myself, might seek a space in the back where dozing would be less noticed, or so we thought.

Trying to remain unnoticed was my challenge, but I think my ability to blend in with the Republican Brotherhood, and not be constantly treated as the "American other," was a good part of my attraction to the organization. Although there was certainly considerable commentary from the brothers about my different appearance, they focused primarily on their perception of my becoming like them, even in appearance. *"inta begait asmar"* (your color is turning "asmar"), was an expression I heard a lot from these multihued people as I picked up a tan. I'm not sure that "asmar" is translatable, but let's say it was their favorite color—and kind of the standard brown that described most people's complexions. I probably (almost) fit in color-wise because the Sudanese have an astonishing array of color names that they use to describe themselves including green, yellow, red, white, blue, and black! But I will also attribute my fitting in to my discretion. I *wanted* to be like them, and I kept quiet and studied their behavior so I could do so. I was impressed with how they treated each other, and I wanted to share in that.

That is not to say there were not tensions. As I have said, I was aware of the terrible human rights abuses occurring all over Sudan, in that era, particularly in the South. But the Republican effort to work on equality and justice as part of their rhetoric as well as their personal agendas impressed me. Nevertheless, it was a surprise when I became aware of ethnic tensions in the house. I was and am a student of Africa and like to have maps of the continent around me. The walls of our house were fairly devoid of decoration so I taped my big map of Africa up on the wall of the room where I usually slept. It proved to be a fascinating exercise as brothers stopped to study it, looking at Sudan in relationship to the rest of the continent, admiring how the country appeared to be the "heart" if Africa was visualized as a human body (do people in every African country think that their country is Africa's heart?). In a quiet moment one of the brothers came up to me and told me, "Steve, I really appreciate that you love Africa." I replied, a bit confused, "Well, here we are in Africa—all of us. I guess we should love it." He continued, "But I have a special reason why I'm happy that you love Africa, which I'll share with you sometime." He was intriguing me, and I asked him about it a couple of days later when we were both away from the house on the University of Khartoum campus. He told me that he was "fellata," which I knew was the local expression to describe the migrants in Sudan from West Africa, northern Nigeria particularly. For generations Hausa and other West Africans crossed the Sahel through Sudan making their way as pilgrims to Mecca. Families often stopped in Sudan and worked as farm laborers in the Gezira, to raise the money to continue their journeys. Many of them just settled in Sudan where there were today entire villages, particularly in the Sennar area, made up of descendants of West African migrants.

This brother's difference was not obvious to me; his Arabic was as perfect as that of any member of the household. As I said above, the Sudanese around me referred to themselves in a dizzying array of colors. But clearly he felt some discrimination, which I grew to understand came from the "Arab Sudanese" strong orientation toward the "Middle East" as their cultural zone, not Africa. This also explained the fascination with my Africa map, and I also looked at Sudan secondary school geography texts where Middle Eastern countries were featured far more prominently than Africa, despite Sudan's location. As the American historian of Sudan Jay Spaulding explained, Sudan's fifteenth-century Funj Kingdom adopted Islam and Arabic as the state religion and language almost simultaneously, to raise the prestige of the regime. Ethnically and appearance-wise, the closest regional relatives of the northern Sudanese are the nearby

Ethiopians and Eritreans, not the peoples of the Arabian Peninsula. I often think about Dr. Asma Abdelhalim's comment to me while she was doing her doctorate at Ohio University and spent time in our African Studies Program, where students from twenty to thirty African countries are often represented. "We Sudanese, Steve, come to study Africa here with you, and we understand for the first time that we are African." The identity issue has raged in Sudan throughout its history, and has fueled all of its political violence. I also remember watching the news on Sudan television over the years and observing with the brothers how the news readers in describing Sudan's foreign relations with nearby countries would always refer to a link between Sudan and an "Arab" or Muslim country as *been al biladain a-shageegain* (between the brotherly nations), while those between Sudan and, say, Kenya or Ethiopia, *been al biladain a-sadeegain* (between the friendly nations). These attitudes contributed to pushing South Sudan out of the Republic, and the bloody turmoil continues. One of the difficult ironies in this situation is the racist discrimination that Sudanese face from their "Arab brothers." Sudanese who travel to Saudi Arabia and its neighboring Gulf countries to work often experience racism there, with many reporting hearing the epithet, *abid,* slave, within earshot. Of course, the name Sudan itself was bestowed by the Arabs who referred to the entire African region as *bilaad as-sudan,* "land of the blacks."

While I may have sought a place on a mat at the rear of the evening's jelsa, I did in fact always feel like I had a front row seat to observe—and occasionally participate in—Islamic social change. The leaders of the organization, men and women selected by Ustadh Mahmoud for their spiritual strength and understanding of the Republican ideology, were supportive of my presence among the brothers. But I did feel a bit shy toward the senior leaders, and perhaps slightly intimated by their serious outlook—at least initially—and drew my own support and knowledge of the movement from the brothers around me in the house. This latter group also became the best source in the wider Republican community for "understanding Steve's accent," and they often offered to translate my version of Sudanese Arabic for anyone needing this service. The brothers' house is where I did learn the language that has allowed me to share this experience and to cross the threshold of other doorways, including the home of Ustadh Mahmoud.

Lunch at the "brothers' house" in Atbara, wafd trip of 1982

"Hajja Rhoda." Rhoda Abdullahi and her husband, Mohamed El
Hassan Mohamed Khair, Rufa'a, 1982

Ustadh Khalid El Haj, in Wad el Fadl, eastern Gezira, 1989

Winter farming of ajur, cucumber, Blue Nile near Rufa'a

Tombs of saints (awlia) in the old cemetery at Abu Haraz, Blue Nile

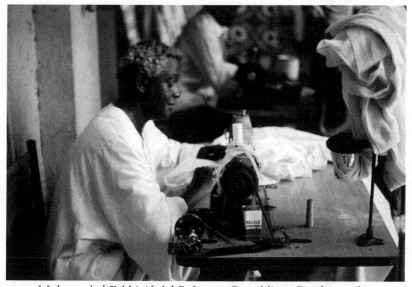

Mohamed el Fekki Abdel Rahman, Republican Brother, tailor

Amna Lotfi, wife of Mahmoud Mohamed Taha

Somaya Mahmoud, Taha's daughter, working in Showak, eastern Sudan

Republican families strolling with author on the banks of the
Atbara River, eastern Sudan

Somaya Mahmoud with her mother, Amna Lotfi

Ustadh Mahmoud officiating at a Republican wedding, ca. 1975

Mahmoud Mohamed Taha, ca. 1975

Brothers and sisters gathered with Ustadh Mahmoud
in front of his house, ca. 1980

Bus ride in Cairo, Talab Zahran with Melaz Mohammed-al-Fatih

4
A Women's Movement

August generally brings rain to the Khartoum region, replacing the hot, clear sky with thick orange clouds reflecting the baked clay earth below. I remember those orange clouds against the blue sky on the day of Am Fadl's funeral. He was old and had been ill for some time, wheelchair-bound. *Am* ("Uncle," a common honorific for an older man) Mohamed Fadl had been one of Ustadh Mahmoud's original followers, from the time of the pre-independence Republican Party. He bridged the colonial and independent Sudan eras, working as a teacher and a school inspector in Omdurman, and both of his daughters, Nawal and Rashida, were prominent Republican Sisters as well. News of his death spread quickly through the Republican community, and everyone who was able converged on Ustadh Mahmoud's house to share condolences. Although many of the brothers had been explaining to me the Republican Brotherhood's progressive philosophy about women's place in Islam, the preparations and burial of Am Fadl that followed gave me my first opportunity to witness the Republican women apply what they had learned from Ustadh Mahmoud on the front lines of Islamic transformation. Every aspect of the women's new lives as Republicans was a rebuke to Muslim convention that kept women from full participation in the life of the Muslim community (ummah). The death of Am Fadl introduced me to the drama that accompanied this transformation.

As a single, male, young foreigner—whose Arabic was less than nuanced at that point—my access to Sudanese women in general and the Republican Sisters specifically was limited, although, according to some of the brothers, I was developing a specialty of talking to grandmothers. Grandmothers always had time to talk to me, and they taught me new vocabulary. I also had good rapport with the women in the households of my closest friends. All of the other sisters treated me with kindness, good humor, and understanding if not considerable curiosity. When we did have conversations, I found the sisters to be articulate spokespersons for Republican thinking. I also believed that the women viewed me as a potential source of information of what went on exactly in the female-less brothers' houses, particularly in the arenas of cooking and cleaning. In any case, the events surrounding Am Fadl's death and burial allowed me to view up close many of the struggles that women faced, unfolding against the backdrop of social tensions in urban Omdurman. Death is a public phenomenon in this culture, and the emotions it reveals trump family privacy.

Following death, the imperative in Islam is to get the body of the deceased into the ground as quickly as possible, ideally before the sun sets on that day. The hot climate of Sudan makes this Qur'anic injunction all the more vivid. Am Fadl's remains were transported from the hospital where he had died to his home on Mourada, the riverside thoroughfare in Omdurman; the name Mourada actually refers to a river port. When the pickup truck from the hospital arrived at the gate to Am Fadl's family home, there was a group of his women relatives and neighbors there to begin the mourning. In Sudan women are boxed into the customs of "popular Islam," that is, the nonorthodox practices that characterize the cultural margins of the Muslim community.

Women outside of the Republican community were generally not entirely expected to keep up with the obligations of prayer or expected to know much of the Qur'an, for example. Or they participated in "cults," like *zar*, which was a practice of magic and charms common across the Horn of Africa and had pre-Islamic origins. At the gate to Am Fadl's house these non-Republican women wailed theatrically and tried to grab the wrapped corpse from the hands of the brothers who were bringing it into the house for the ritual washing. I had never seen this custom before and found it unsettling, having largely been protected from this Sudanese reality in my new life among the Republicans, or in my old one in the United States, for that matter. But the point of pretending to grab the corpse was that the women "wouldn't accept death's reality." And the women who wailed the loudest or grabbed with the most gusto were supposed to be perceived as the most deeply grieving. Islamic orthodoxy would of course dictate that what followed death—heaven, *al-akhira*—was an improvement over life on earth. But women were thought to be obsessed with life's material things and less interested in the disposition of their souls. (I was always amused to hear the tales of restless *ba'ati,* souls coming back from the dead, who were thought to be women searching for the household items—pots, pans—which they had accumulated while alive. I don't recall anyone ever relating one of these tales to me, however, with a straight face. My friend and Republican sister, and daughter of the deceased, Nowal Fadl, told me that when she became a Republican she actually gave away her jewelry to try to counter this image of rapacious women.)

The washing of Am Fadl's remains and the preparation for burial took place in a room just off the main entrance to the house. The Republicans took pride in maintaining these religiously required rituals, and they had been concerned enough about sustaining the knowledge of the details that they had published a book on the proper steps and prayers in this ritual, which became a Republican best seller. Some of the younger brothers were invited inside to observe and learn the washing ritual and prayers themselves as the body was shrouded and placed on a new angareb, the traditional woven sisal bed with ornately tooled legs painted bright red.

Meanwhile, a quickly growing crowd of brothers and sisters was gathered inside the house, spilling out from the saloon to the verandas of the house and finding seats on mats on the floor if not beds that had been moved from around the house to provide seating for as many as possible. They sang the Republican hymns, *inshad,* whose words covered both the theology and the theological heritage of the movement—with different brothers and sisters, both those with significant musical chops and those with a great deal of soul, taking turns at leading the group. All of the assembled mourners joined in the chorus.

Finally the *jenaza,* Am Fadl's shrouded remains, was brought out lying on the angareb. Four brothers took the legs of the bed, hoisted it onto their shoulders, and carried it out the gate and on to the street as pallbearers. The wailing outside of the gate reached its apex while the Republicans inside looked stoic or deeply saddened. The house emptied of the Republican mourners, who fell in line three or four abreast behind the lofted angareb. During the discussions among the movement leadership that had taken place while the body was prepared for burial, they made a historic decision that the sisters would for the first time join the procession to the cemetery. Women in Sufi Sudan spent a great deal of time in cemeteries visiting the tombs of saints and their own departed family members, but custom effectively forbade their attendance at burials. This custom was an extension of the idea that men and women did not pray together, a major requirement of the actual burial—women being seen as an unacceptable distraction to men at prayer.

Women's full participation in all of Islam's obligations was one of Mahmoud Mohamed Taha's most important goals in establishing his movement. He moved to accomplish these goals by instilling in his followers the confidence that this was the reality deigned by God which required us to actualize it; it was not something to strategize about. The method was to follow in the Prophet's path and to assert the right to focus on that lofty road was the only permission required.

But that is not to diminish the courage demonstrated by the sisters in joining the Republican men in the masira, the procession to the cemetery. The women followed discreetly, bunched together in their flowing white garments at the end of the line, careful not to mix with the men and at an appropriate distance from them. We had to walk through the narrow streets of neighborhoods en route and one of the brothers began the dhikkir chant of Allah! Allah! effectively pacing the marching mourners as they made their way through Omdurman. Children were always attracted to this type of event, an everyday occurrence in densely populated Omdurman with its many cemeteries. But usually funeral processions moved quietly and quickly through the streets, the only words being spoken by those seeking the baraka /blessing of taking a turn bearing a leg of the angareb as it was otherwise passed silently among the male mourners. In this case the spectacle of the chanting men and women marching together drew people out of their houses or stopped them on the street to stare, laugh, or glare at the women's flouting of convention.

It was the hottest part of an August afternoon when the procession reached the Hammad a-Nil cemetery, a mile or so from Am Fadl's home on Mourada. Particularly in urban Sudan, cemeteries are closely surrounded by neighborhood housing, and it is not uncommon to walk through the dusty burial ground to get from one part of the neighborhood to another. These sites are not maintained with any special care, a perspective linked to concerns of idolatry that were banished by Islam's revelation in the seventh century. Many cemeteries in Sufi Sudan, including this one, feature at least one qubba or Turkish-style tomb of a wali, a Sufi teacher of a particular sect whose teachings are remembered as keys to a good spiritual life and heaven's gate. But as we spot a sun-blanched femur or hip bone in the dust we are reminded of our limited time on earth.

Men readied the burial place for Am Fadl as the angareb was brought to rest in an open spot reserved for the *salat-a-jenaza,* the communal prayer that immediately precedes burial. A bladed tool was swung back and forth by two men to open a grave in the dusty earth. Ustadh Mahmoud had been driven to the cemetery and now stood beside his late shrouded friend, trying to protect him from the sun by holding his white shawl as a shade over the body. The brothers lined up facing the qibla, the direction of prayer, and in an unprecedented move, the sisters lined up behind the men at some distance to join in the prayer.

Unless they are husband and wife, men and women generally do not pray together in Islam, and particularly not at a burial. The sisters joining in the salat-a-jenaza was a provocative act and yet one that was a somewhat restrained statement. There were not many people near the cemetery on that hot afternoon, and the burial prayer does not feature prostration. The mourners stand in their shoe-clad feet as the basic prayers are recited. The important role that Am Fadl had played throughout Ustadh Mahmoud's career meant that he did not want any member of the Republican family to be excluded from the community event marking the end of his friend and colleague's life on earth.

Despite these justifications, the sight of women joining in the cemetery burial prayer did provoke a small group of men, some of those non-Republicans who had been preparing the burial site itself, to climb up into the bed of a pickup truck and begin to lob stones at the line of praying women, more to disturb them than hurt them. The seriousness of this affront to women at prayer may be measured by the lengths to which one Muslim will not interfere with another who is engaged in the act of praying. People are careful to walk behind a person at prayer so as to not disturb him or her, and would certainly never try to speak to a person praying. The concept of hudur, "presence" or intense concentration, defines how prayer is best performed, and how it is its most beneficial to the believer.

My own hudur at prayer was obviously broken by this violent act; otherwise, I would not be reporting it here. But the sisters did not flinch as they performed what they saw as their duty as believing Muslims, and when I asked various participants about it later, no one would confirm my story. But no one denied it had happened either. Ustadh Mahmoud taught his followers that Republican fikr (ideology) was to be put into practice not for the purpose of public demonstration, but to strengthen one's own spiritual capacity. And this was certainly neither the first or last time that Republicans' manifestations of their spiritual perspectives were met with violence.

To be a Republican Sister was to validate the premise of gender equality that was the core teaching of *The Second Message of Islam:* "Islam's original precept is complete equality between men and women," as he wrote in that book. Mahmoud Mohamed Taha was consistent and unwavering on this position, from Sudan's late colonial period through the coups and rare democratic regimes post-independence, through the national experiments with various development schemes, and the absorption of Sudan into the trends of global Islam. The women of the movement demonstrated with courage and enthusiasm in their daily lives that they were included in Mahmoud Mohamed Taha's claim that Islam would achieve freedom for every human being, and that the sisters in fact were the ultimate examples of the Republican ideology under the circumstances of Sudanese patriarchy. The sisters were not an auxiliary to the men's movement or a parallel organization, but rather, they traveled together with the brothers on the Path of the Prophet. Equality for Muslim men and women was a central goal of this Islamic revival movement rather than a by-product. Women's counting less than men in social or legal terms was not a possible outcome in the fulfillment of Mahmoud Mohamed Taha's promise; the sisters' experience provided the best opportunity to implement Taha's effort to "evolve sharia." As Republican Sister and University of Khartoum student leader Awatif Abdel Gadir told me, "We were the reason for this movement; we owned the issue." The Republican women would not be denied their identification as fully engaged modern Muslims, and the entire Republican organization was dedicated to that cause. The development of women, in Taha's view, began with the development of their souls through egalitarian engagement in reviving Islam.

To be a modern woman from a Republican perspective was to be a Republican Muslim woman, on a path to self-realization. Many times Republican sisters told me in interviews that the Republican ideology helped them "find themselves." Some of the leaders who were sisters tried to explain to me that to be modern was to have the capacity to reach so far inside prayer that the answers to life's dilemmas became clearer; that the capacity for humans to unravel the meaning of the Qur'an was within reach. And then one could begin to address those problems as they affected the community, as the Prophet Mohamed was said to have done. Achieving equality with men was only the beginning of that modernity, but an important first step. The religious training and immersion in an Islamic intellectualism were keys to achieving that goal, keys that provided the sisters with both the spiritual and temporal sense of progress through human history. It put the sisters in an odd place in the context of Sudan societal expectations of women.

The traditional view of women's spiritual life in Sudan is fixed on the expectation that women will obey God and essentially not interfere with men's practice of their religion. The religious restrictions placed on women, about modesty in dress, where they may worship in mosques, where their voices may and may not be heard, women's obligations in marriage, and so on are more about assuring that men not be distracted from their spiritual lives than about cultivating that spirit in women. It seemed to me that the general view of women in Sudan was that they were more superstitious than religious.

Sudan's modernity gap was brought into focus for Mahmoud Mohamed Taha by female circumcision, a practice fueled by women's lack of access to education. The ancient custom allowed the British to label colonial Sudan as "primitive and backward" in Taha's view in order to stall the move toward the country's independence, which I discussed in chapter 1. Victorian images of Muslim women as oppressed and in need of liberation had been commonplace during the early British occupation of both Sudan and Egypt and served in part to justify colonization. The elimination of female circumcision was so central to Taha's vision of modern Sudan that he wrote about it in the Republican Party's "First Booklet," published in 1945, the only pre-independence party manifesto at the time to mention female circumcision, and indeed, Taha's only mention of violence in a long life of struggle. The pamphlet's rhetoric said, referring to the British colonizers, "We will defeat you with blood and sparks."[1] Equality between men and women was consistent with Taha's anticolonial idea of equality among all the peoples of the world as the solution to oppression. His campaign to eliminate female circumcision was characteristic of his search for sustainable approaches to evolve Sudanese culture and society. As religion could not be imposed on people, nor could social change; it had to come from within.

A Women's-Rights Culture

It could be said that Mahmoud Mohamed Taha's most significant contribution to twentieth-century African social history was his linkage of the elevation of the status of women to the political, cultural, and religious development of the continent. That Mahmoud Mohamed Taha could found and lead an organization in which the women members could feel included in its mission, while its male members understood that the promotion of a women's-rights agenda was part of men's liberation as well as their religious obligation, ibada, was another remarkable achievement. On a visit to Athens, Ohio, Republican sister Ikhlas Himet told me that Ustadh Mahmoud had said, "There was never a religious society for women before the Republican community; women had neglected their human/religious potential, and Sharia won't let women progress." The task of total inclusion of women in the Republican project was a tremendous burden for the entire movement, in that religious inclusion ran counter to the wider society's views on women and religion. I often noted that the goal of inclusion was not necessarily embraced with vigor by all of the Brothers with the same degree of enthusiasm as their Sisters. It was a learning project for the men as well, who were making a huge adjustment in their worldview. As the entire Republican organization resisted the imposed authority of Islamic orthodoxy, the Republican women resisted the imposition of authority on them by their male colleagues in the struggle to support Mahmoud Mohamed Taha's strong position.

The Republican position on women's rights in Islam was frequently the target of everything from fatwas (legal opinions) from Sudanese and Egyptian *ulema,* to annoying harassment and insults in the streets of Khartoum that included the sisters having their hair and clothing pulled. But Mahmoud Mohamed Taha and his followers remained committed to their agenda with relentless energy and a deep understanding that to leave women behind was not possible in their quest for absolute individual freedom. If women were not free, no one could be free was the consistent pledge of Ustadh Mahmoud's teaching.

I think it is useful to try to explain here the philosophical points developed by Ustadh Mahmoud that were what the sisters and brothers were trying to live up to in their lives. The situation of women in society was a core value of Taha's work in his book *The Second Message of Islam.* He wrote, "Social philosophy throughout the ages, up to and including contemporary communism, has failed to appreciate the relationship between the individual and the community. It has assumed if the individual found the opportunity to exercise his freedom, his activity would go against the interest of the community. As the community was considered to be greater than the individual, then its interest deserved to be put before those of the individual. Hence, the freedom of the individual was curtailed in the interest of the community whenever it appeared that the two were inconsistent."[2] The individual, of particular interest here despite the gendered possessive pronoun, is woman. In the sense of Islam's "first message" community of Medina, women were not yet ready to accept the responsibility of their freedom, according to Taha. They had been granted equality with men in the Meccan revelations of the Qur'an, but these "original precepts" as Taha calls them—rights to divorce, equality with men, no polygamy, no gender segregation, and no required veiling—were withdrawn in the "transitional stage" of human development represented by the Prophet's community at Medina. Freedoms were curtailed during the Medinan stage of Mohamed's Prophecy because as Taha wrote in *The Second Message of Islam,* the "prevailing circumstances" of the unsettled and violent Medinan epoch required more social control.

The crucial verse of the Qur'an revealed during the Medina phase of Mohamed's Prophecy is from the chapter titled "The Woman":

> *a-Nisa: Men are the guardians and maintainers of women, because God has endowed one with more [strength] than the other, and because they spend of their means [on them]. Therefore the righteous women are obedient, guarding in secret that which God would have them guard. As to those to women on whose part ye fear disloyalty and ill-conduct, admonish them and banish them to separate beds, and beat them. Then*

as they obey you, seek not a way against them. For God is exalted, Great. (4:34)

The verse is well known for its use of the term "guardian" and in Arabic, *al-giwama* continues today as the term to code male-female relationships in Islamic societies, the scriptural justification for gender inequality. When Muslim men today speak of their wives obeying them as part of women's "ibada," this verse is the source of that understanding. The verse was revealed during the time when women, in Taha's words, were not "ready to properly discharge the duties of freedom," although he continues, "Early Islamic legislation was, in fact, a great leap forward for women, in comparison to their previous status. Nevertheless, it was far below Islam's ultimate objective [of complete equality between men and women],"[3] which is represented in the Meccan verses of the Qur'an, that is, the "second message" of Islam. Progress, in Taha's interpretation, is made through engagement of the texts, a process in which he carefully included his women followers. He taught them to emulate the Prophet's practice, which he believed would lead to complete equality between men and women.

Women were making their way in the modern world, in Taha's view, and he pointed out the irony of their continued oppression by the sharia observed as law by many Muslim societies. He wrote, "We have today in Khartoum a female judge in Shari'a law with her degree from the Faculty of Law in Khartoum. This means that she will take care of the application of the Islamic Shari'a for those who ask for her decision, and she has a right to do this in the same way as those who graduated with her. But the same Shari'a rules say that if this female judge should appear as a witness her testimony would count only half of the testimony from any man in the street. Is this sensible talk? No indeed! This absurdity is not part of religion. The absurdity comes from those brains that refuse to see the contradiction in this, who refuse to understand that there is a cause, a very simple cause. The cause is that the Shari'a law of our fathers had as its mission to serve community in a certain period as a transitional instrument, and it is unable to function in front of the needs of modern times."[4] He continued, "When they [women] have attained the level of self-control and self-protection the guardianship of men will be revoked and cancelled, as it will be left to themselves under the guidance of God to take care of their own matters, under the guardianship of the law."[5]

Women have evolved in modern times, in Taha's view, and are ready to take on the responsibilities implied in the quest for human freedom. Rather than write specifically about what women should do in these modern times, Taha focused in his writing on what the Path of the Prophet prescribed, and then encouraged the sisters to demonstrate their ability to follow that path and his surrogates to talk about it in public. But from his relationships with the sisters it was clear that he knew their capacity, and he rewarded its expansion with increasing responsibility in Republican campaigns to revive Islam. Ultimately he permitted his two daughters and his niece, among other sisters, to confront the Nimeiry regime's planned imposition of "Islamic law" by speaking out, getting arrested and being detained for twelve months in the Omdurman Women's Prison, between 1983 and 1984. The senior leaders' sisters, such as Taha's niece and the city government administrator Batoul Mokhtar, worked with the other sisters to understand the Qur'an and Taha's writings and apply those texts in participating in all of the activities of the movement, in which they all demonstrated a great deal of excitement and responsibility. The sisters' earnest participation in every phase of Republican campaigns to change Sudanese society made women's advancement the priority issue even for the Republican men.

The Republican men took their role in the campaign for women's advancement very seriously and sought means to communicate the effort to the wider society. Ahmed Dali, the leading

Republican public speaker, explained to me the evolutionary approach that he took to try to persuade his difficult and largely male audiences: "I told them that your fathers pushed fifty years ago to get girls into primary school. Now they are doctors and judges. Many of them no longer have material or economic dependence on you. And with modern technology women don't even depend on us for our strength. I would tell the audience that men need to evolve, too." What Sudan had accomplished for women, in the Republican view was the foundation for its modernity. Dali echoed his teacher as he tried to get his male audiences to see that they were ready to live in the era of the Second Message of Islam.

The intellectual was always deeply intertwined with the emotional on the level of Ustadh Mahmoud's relationships with the sisters. A brother illustrated for me the deep bond between Ustadh Mahmoud and the sisters with an incident from Taha's final imprisonment, a difficult period that came at a time when the sisters had been starting to feel the power of faith learned from their teacher as well as the deep sense of loss of the daily inspiring contact with him. After his arrest in June 1983 Ustadh Mahmoud was held alone under house-arrest conditions in a building at state security police headquarters in Khartoum. But in an indefatigably Sudanese informal manner, from time to time he was allowed to have medical appointments outside of detention, and would be driven to the appointment by one of his followers accompanied by security police. The brother with the driving assignment would alert Republicans to the route so that they could stand outside and at least see their teacher in the car.

As they made their way to the doctor's office in a military hospital, the car passed one of the sisters, Suad Sulaiman, standing by the road clutching her son, Mahmoud, then about one year old. For an unknown reason, the brother driving managed to stop the car, although I will guess that the accompanying security police officer was sympathetic to the cause of family ties.

Ustadh Mahmoud was able to take the child from Suad and hug him very close, while his mother stood silently with her hands clasped together touching her forehead in a gesture of deep appreciation and understanding. She later told me it had felt as if she herself had been embraced by Ustadh Mahmoud.

"Binaati mu'alafaati"

The deep understanding that promoted communication between the sisters and Ustadh Mahmoud was a product of education. The expression *binaati mu'alafaati*, "my daughters (women followers) are my writings," was used by Ustadh Mahmoud to indicate that women's spiritual growth was a key output of his project to revive Islam. It is a paraphrase of the Egyptian Sufi master, As-Shadhali (d. 1258 CE) who referred to his followers as embodying his knowledge; in Ustadh Mahmoud's usage we sense the individual care he gave to ensuring the success of his project as well as to the recruitment process. It was clear that there was *formation* involved in becoming a Republican sister through the practice of Ustadh Mahmoud's teachings.

Some were born into the movement, as was the elder daughter of Ustadh Mahmoud, Asma. And yet her story is emblematic of the condition of women in Sudan and how far the Republican ideology took her in changing that condition, step by careful step.

We grew up in Rufa'a in the home of my maternal grandfather while Ustadh Mahmoud was busy with establishing the movement in Khartoum," she told me. "In those days (early 1950s) we girls could only go out to go to school during the day, not to visit friends or go to the market or anything like that. We could only go out visiting after dark—because during the daylight hours if men saw us or we saw men, that would be shameful to our families. But I imagined sometimes that I was part of a women's movement; I wasn't sure why or how, but I had this feeling that that was what I wanted to do.

During my secondary school years I started to spend school holidays with Ustadh Mahmoud in Khartoum. And then I started to see life's possibilities and what freedom could be.

I became seriously involved with the movement around 1970. When Ustadh Mahmoud announced that it was time for the sisters to join the brothers out on the Republican book-selling and discussion campaigns in the streets of Khartoum, some of the brothers complained, and we sisters were afraid as well. We knew we would encounter the fanatics and all the questions and stares on the streets. And the brothers were worried that they would have to spend all their time protecting us. Prior to this new idea that we would participate in the book sales, the sisters would spend the time that the brothers were out on sales sitting at the home of Ustadh Mahmoud reading and discussing the Republican books, which we eventually engaged in selling. We also worked on learning Qur'an and learning its meaning. If we were to go out on the streets not fully armed with this knowledge, it would be just like some political movement where you depend on your colleague's information to carry things along and not on yourself. So finally, when we did go out onto to the streets of Khartoum to sell the Republican books, we were ready for any question. The first few times that the sisters went out on sales a team of brothers lurked behind each group of us."

Omer El Garrai told me details from the incident of Ustadh Mahmoud's sending the sisters out for book selling for the first time. "The brothers protested, saying that they could not protect the sisters on the streets, and Ustadh Mahmoud told us, 'You are not afraid for the sisters' safety; you are afraid of equality with the sisters." But we brothers sold no books on those first few nights when the sisters were selling; we were too busy watching for their safety. And the sisters' sales of books were tremendous!"

I asked Asma Mahmoud how she believed women became so central to the agenda of the Republican Brotherhood.

It was something spiritual. Before the episode with the midwife in Rufa'a—she had been arrested by the British for circumcising a young girl—the situation of women had not been on the agenda of Ustadh Mahmoud' politics. I think it was like his experience in spiritual isolation [khalwa] later in Rufa'a where he thought about the essence of the "second message of Islam." He had been at the mosque that day and heard about the arrest of the woman, and it just came to him that he needed to do something. His arrest following that demonstration led to his eventual spiritual seclusion exercise, and the thinking that came with his understanding of the "second message." So, I think it was spiritual power that led to women finding a place in the Republican ideology.

Asma Mahmoud and some of her sister Republicans were also among the first female political prisoners in Sudan,[6] a period of detention that they came to view as important exposure to women's reality in their country. The circumstances that the sisters faced were very different than those of the large group of brothers who were similarly detained at that time, the 1983–85 crackdown on the Republican Brotherhood. The brothers were held in the political section of "Kober" Prison in Khartoum North where they were treated as politicians with special foods, relatively comfortable quarters, and so on. Sudan had little experience with female political prisoners, so there was no special section for them. Asma and her sisters were thrown in with prostitutes and the poor women brewers of merisa, the mildly alcoholic sorghum beverage that had become illegal under Nimeiry's sharia code.

Asma told me, "We saw the circumstances of poor women's lives while we were in prison, what they had to do to take care of their families. Some of the women were there because they had killed their husbands, after being beaten. And it was a very important time for us for our ibada [personal spiritual conduct]. We sang our religious poetry, read Republican books, took a long time with our ablutions, and prayed so much. We also taught some of the other women how to read and about their obligations as Muslim women. We got inside ourselves a bit."[7] Asma and the other Republican sisters had been arrested for speaking out in anticipation of Nimeiry's sharia laws, which many understood to sanction wife beating under the Qur'anic verse of guardianship, 4:34, and Sudan cultural norms.

Republican women learned to stand up for themselves in other arenas as well; they often found themselves on the front lines—alone—enduring indignities and representing Republican ideals that were at such odds with the wider society. I got to know sister Nowal Fadl and her husband well when they invited me to stay with them in their Cairo apartment in exile from Sudan in the early 1990s. Nowal related an incident from when she attended a technical training course in Germany. "There was an event at the Sudan Embassy to which all the Sudanese students had been invited. I met about twenty of my countrymen there, and it came time for the sunset prayer. I was ready to pray when the Imam, a senior Sudanese man, came and greeted all the men with a handshake. When I offered my hand, he refused it with a gruff, 'I have done my ablutions' [implying that he could not break his "purity" by shaking a woman's hand]. I was shocked and snapped back with 'But I too have performed my ablutions!'" The perceived impurity or distractive powers of women are in part behind arguments for veiling, for their exclusion from praying with men, and for limiting their public participation in some societies.

The strands of Mahmoud Mohamed Taha's project to develop women—that their spiritual competence was sure, that they could speak in public about what they knew, that they shared responsibility with the brothers, that they grew in learning and professions—were layered in over time and eventually could not be separated from one another, creating one strong cord of activist faith. Getting to know these women, their histories of struggles and indignities, was an important part of my feeling in Sudan like I was on the front line of African social change.

Women in White

The sisters' house, *beyt-al-ukhwat,* was an institution unique to the Republican organization. Religious organizations in Sudan, including the many Sufi sects, generally did not provide accommodation for their women members. But in the spirit of equality, in that brothers' houses were established in Thawra near the home of Ustadh Mahmoud for men, there needed to be a facility for sisters as well. At any one time about a dozen Republican sisters lived at the home of Mahmoud Mohamed Taha under circumstances very different from that of the brothers' houses. The sisters did not have a space of their own but shared their living space with the entire organization in that when they rose early in the morning to begin their days, they had to make sure all of their bedding and clothing and so on were packed away. In a few moments the space where they had slept and prayed would become the room where Ustadh Mahmoud met with his followers all day long. And if a general meeting went late into the night, that meant delaying the sister residents' time for sleep as well.

The sisters living at the home of Ustadh Mahmoud were generally students or unmarried working women intensely interested in getting as close as possible to the Republican ideology. The brothers had each other and the senior Republicans among them to call on when questions about Islamic texts or the conduct of Republican life came up. But the sisters living in the sisters' house had the highest role model in Ustadh Mahmoud himself, who generally made himself available at all times for their questions or to just listen to their Qur'an reading or spiritual poetry. This also meant that while the brothers' houses, although serious communities, could also be relaxed places of tremendous laughter, the sisters' house had to be circumspect at all times because of the mixed atmosphere of men and women guests in the house at all hours of the day. Their house was also movement headquarters, which affected the atmosphere as well. But it was also the family home of Mahmoud Mohamed Taha, which made it easier for "independent women" to live there. Rising levels of education for women in Sudan were only beginning to change attitudes about women living on their own, even in urban areas. Otherwise, it was most common for women to leave the homes of their fathers for their husbands with no time spent outside of men's "guardianship."

The sisters' house was in effect the Republican leadership training academy for women where the sister residents and visiting sisters could perfect their knowledge of the Qur'an and the writings of Ustadh Mahmoud and other Republicans, as well as to practice what they would say at general meetings of the movement or out on the street with the public. As Nowal Fadl told me, "There was so much controversy over women participating on the front lines of an Islamic organization that we couldn't afford to make mistakes when speaking outside about Islam or the movement's perspective." When the women did take an opportunity to speak and participate in group discussions, it was always in a thoughtful manner. Nowal continued, "Becoming a Republican helped me find my voice," an impression shared by many of the women who chose the Republican path. Another sister, Selwa Ahmed el Bedawi, said that the house was like the khalwa where Ustadh Mahmoud had perfected his thinking on the second message of Islam. "We learned how to follow the Path of the Prophet there; we prayed, talked, slept, washed, read, and ate around the Path of the Prophet."

This careful apprenticeship to the Republican ideology, particularly for the women, signaled the challenge of becoming a Republican sister and may also have been a reason for the modest numbers of women who followed this path. The expectation that the women would learn Qur'an and its interpretations, be able to discuss fine points of the Republican ideology, and follow its rigorous practice of prayer kept all but the most committed women away from the movement. The sisters were predominantly the daughters and wives of Republicans, but there were also many sisters who joined from the teaching professions, like the men. Primary and secondary education and instructors in the teacher training institutes were important sources of recruitment for the Republican sisterhood. Republicans were very proud of their members who were women in professions like medicine and the law, although they were few in number. Ustadh Mahmoud took time to mark the graduations of all these women, announcing at meetings that their scholastic achievements were important events in the history of the movement.

Awatif Abdel Gadir joined the movement because she had expressed women's rights notions to her family as a teenager, and one day her older brother brought her home some Republican publications to read. In 1975 the Brotherhood published a yearlong series of books commemorating the first International Women's Year; the series received wide circulation. At the University of Khartoum Awatif Abdel Gadir ran for the Student Union and won a seat, although the organization had been dominated by Muslim Brotherhood members for six years prior to her election. She started to speak publicly on campus about the Republican ideology, and the backlash from opposition organizations produced a strong letter (see below) from Ustadh Mahmoud defending the rights of the Republican Sisters. The extraordinary concern of Ustadh Mahmoud for this issue is noted in the fact that at this stage of his leadership of the Republican Brotherhood he rarely made public interactions with those outside of his organization:

A Women's Movement

I have received your invitation to participate in your Second Cultural Season, and I thank you for that. The Republican ideology is a Sudanese ideology with regard to its home. It is an authentic idea that has no peer in the Islamic thought throughout its long history. It has, in addition to that, its history and achievement in educating young boys and girls who are now conducting a great and unique role in our contemporary history: the role of spreading Islamic awareness among our people by open, logical, trustful, and brave discussions in liberal platforms held on public grounds in different towns and the University. This idea and this phenomenon—the phenomenon of free platforms— are really new, especially when we consider the debate on religion as the experience of the young Sudanese woman in these platforms. Both the ideology and the phenomenon of the young woman who appears with this character, this bravery, and this great knowledge attracted the attention of many foreign visitors and were respected and appreciated by them. However, despite that, the ideology and the phenomenon do draw at the university under your leadership nothing but perversion, slander, revilement, and enmity that contradicts the spirit of knowledge and sincere liberal research. Yet you are even more further from the spirit of knowledge and sincere investigation by inviting the enemies of this ideology who delude you and exacerbate your enmity to it. In your inner feeling you wish our speeches to be untrue and this ideology to be false and wrong. A week ago one of your leaders was lecturing you and insisting without any logic or evidence to damn me as an infidel while you are shouting, clapping, and laughing. Under your leadership the university is declining from expected standards with regard to earnestness, science, and freedom of thought and is focusing on regrettable demagogy.

Sincerely, Mahmoud Mohamed Taha.[8]

The increasingly shrill campus Islamic politics of the time drew a proportional response from Ustadh Mahmoud.

Asma Mahmoud remembered her involvement in the recruitment of women, calling the objective the "women's movement" (haraka-t-al-mar'a). "We felt that we had a program aimed at women. I talked to women about their problems and how the Republican ideology would address those problems. I talked to women who had been beaten by their husbands or fathers, even to women who were beaten for thinking about joining our organization!" She also mentioned that they were successful in recruiting some women from the Sudan Communist Party, more than women from other political or religious organizations. The SCP and the Republican organization both encouraged women's activism more than the other groups. There was never, however, a great concern in the Republican Brotherhood about recruitment in terms of increasing the membership of the organization. "The world will understand what we have here some day, and they will come to us" were often-repeated words of Ustadh Mahmoud. Recruitment was always a process that allowed the individual Republican the opportunity to test his or her knowledge of the group's ideology, improving that knowledge whether the recruitment was successful or not.

The Republican sisters approached the controversial issue of Muslim women's dress in a practical and symbolic manner. Their collective identity was marked by the white taub, a gauzy, sari-like garment that was also the uniform of women office workers and teachers, also mourners in Sudan. The taub was loosely wrapped around the body and over one's dress, covering the hair only partially and generally falling below the knee. Today's taub was nine meters of imported polyester, but it was an update of the classic hand-loomed cotton garment worn by rural women in Sudan. The Sudanese convention was that women dressed modestly, but the internationalization of Islam in the country fueled campaigns to cover women up more thoroughly, despite the desert heat of northeast Africa.

The business-like simplicity of the white taub resolved the conflict between women's desire to work, to go out, and the need for modesty. The conflict is clear in the wide variety of clothing that passes for *zei Islami,* "Islamic dress," in Sudan and throughout the Muslim world. Women can be seen today in the close fitting, hair-covering head-gear known as hijab—sometimes in bright colors and/or fastened with glittery jewelry—or a tightly tied scarf around the head, or very loose garments that cover head to toe in an effort to hide body contours. Some women have adopted the totally black covering that also hides the face completely, associated with Gulf mores. The *taub-a-Sudani* would be the only indigenous garment on this list, another reason for its adoption as the Republican sisters' uniform. There was a sense of virtue about wearing it as well; that wearing the taub fulfilled the requirement of Islamic modesty while serving the need for practicality in the life of a busy modern woman. But for the Republican sister the taub's contribution to a woman's modesty was secondary to her virtuous and conscientious behavior.

The taub's significance to the women's movement became clearer to me years later while talking to a Republican sister resident in Doha, Qatar, where a dozen or so Republican women were working and/or accompanying their husbands. I asked Naziha Mohamed el-Hassan why the sisters in Doha were wearing colorful taubs, more associated in Sudan with either at-home wear or what non-Republican women might wear on the street. She replied, "The white taub represents something to us; it is symbolic of our ties to each other as Republican sisters. But here in Doha, its meaning is lost—people would not know why we were wearing white and would not get the point." In fact, Qatari women generally wear long black robes and tight-fitting head gear in public. That the meaning of the Sudanese white taub was lost even in nearby Cairo was evident when I witnessed

Republican sisters shouted at by Egyptian men with cries of "here come the brides!" as they walked through the city in Republican white. I was particularly amazed that the Republican Sisters walking through Cairo dressed in their white taubs drew more attention from Cairenes than I did as I walked alongside them. For the Republicans, the whole issue of zei islami was little more than narrative diversion from the vital work of reforming Muslim society and the place of women in it.

The presence of teams of these white-taubed women on the streets of Khartoum selling Republican books, attending a Republican lecture at a university en masse, marching in a funeral procession, or joining the *dhikir* chanting with the brothers in front of the home of Ustadh Mahmoud was a strong message of solidarity. As the sisters developed in knowledge and practice of the Republican ideology and confidence in speaking about it, honed through meetings at the sisters' house or in *jelsat* (plural of jelsa) with the general Republican congregation, Ustadh Mahmoud gave them more responsibility in representing the movement. Nowal Fadl remembered the first time Ustadh Mahmoud took sisters with him on one of his speaking campaigns, to the northern city of Atbara. As the young women stood behind their teacher during his presentation, he was heckled from the audience with, "Why do you drag your daughters around the countryside? It is shameful!" And Ustadh Mahmoud replied, "I know where my daughters are; do you?"

Although this incident was from the late 1960s, the visible presence of women in public and particularly in an organization with a design for Islamic revival was always a highly sensitive aspect of the women's movement in Sudan. The issue of women covering themselves, of veiling, extended to women's voices in conventional and conservative understanding. The voice of the woman is one "of which one ought to be ashamed" or *awra*, in conventional Islamic understanding. This essentially means that women's voices were to be considered as requiring as much covering up as the rest of their bodies. Ustadh Mahmoud's encouragement of the sisters to speak in public, even publicly chant the spiritual poetry for which the Republicans were known, deliberately fought that convention. But this concern for public perception did have a collective impact on the sisters. Their intense circumspection in their public persona led to a certain stiffness or caution which was not found among the brothers. It was clear that the Republican women were sent out in public as examples to some extent, demonstrating what was possible for women, as in the Uncle Fadl funeral march. But they were deeply proud of the opportunity as well. The women's voices were always the loudest in communal singing or communal reading of a Qur'anic verse. As Asma Mahmoud told me, "We needed to be carefully representing ourselves as Muslim women in public because the wider society was not used to seeing women like us."

But having been granted the freedom by Ustadh Mahmoud's teachings to *be* Muslim women in public was also the cause of their most careful adherence to ibada. I remember talking to two Republican sisters at the Faculty of Education of the University of Khartoum about how their classmates and roommates in the residence halls of the campus were astonished to find that the Republicans would not perform their ablutions in the bathrooms of the dorm, as was the expeditious practice of most, but took an ibreek container filled with water outside to prepare for prayer. "It isn't an inconvenience," one of the sisters told me. "It's what God wants us to do." The sisters were experiencing the power to fully exercise their faith for the first time and approached that power with care, and tried to take good care of it. Awatif Abdel Gadir said, "I loved his freedom," when I asked her why she was devoted to the teachings of Ustadh Mahmoud.

Modern Marriage

Mahmoud Mohamed Taha wrote in *The Reform and Development of the Islamic Personal Law*, "There is something that we can call the real, true marriage. And then we have marriage in Shari'a. In the real, true marriage your wife is the twin for your soul, or a sister. She is an emanation or manifestation or yourself, outside yourself."[9] Taha goes on to make the dramatic point, "We might understand the relation of the wife to her husband implying the same as a man's relation to his God. The wife is the first outpouring of emanation from existing unity to duality."[10] "Relationships with Ustadh Mahmoud were about love," Republican sister Nowal Awad told me. The Republicans developed a comprehensive plan for reform of the basic institution of marriage out of the writings of Mahmoud Mohamed Taha. He frequently spoke of the relationship of marriage as being the most important in society, and the brothers and sisters had him and his wife Umna (our mother) Amna Lotfi, whom he married in 1939, as role models. He wrote, "The criterion of social equality is that marriage [the most fundamental and intimate relation] is possible between any man and any woman. This is the accurate test of social equality."[11] With this philosophy in mind Republicans devised a simple marriage ceremony with a significant impact that eliminated polygamy, frowned on divorce, and almost eliminated the dowry payment. Republican marriage gave women equal rights in the relationship, working toward complete elimination of the guardianship of verse 4:34. It was in the position of marriage that the Republican sisters exercised the full power of the equality they learned in the teachings of Ustadh Mahmoud. The institution of marriage had to be secured as one in which men and women had equal rights if any other element of the Republican ideology was to succeed. In the Republican view the democratically run family as the foundation for a democratic society has been an overlooked element in African and Middle Eastern political theory. As the late Republican Brother Tijani Sadiq told me, "I respect my wife; that is democracy."

The Republican view of marriage was first described in two books by Mahmoud Mohamed Taha, *The Second Message of*

Islam (1967) and *Reform and Development of the Islamic Personal Law* (1971). Consistency continued to be the dominant aspect of Taha's methodology in reviving Islam, which meant that the institution of marriage, the foundation of a stable society, had to be an instrument of human freedom for both husband and wife. *The Second Message of Islam* outlines the differences in the dictates of the First and Second Messages of Islam in regard to polygamy, dowry, and divorce as they pertain to the institution of marriage. Those three elements of spousal interaction were "transitional" in Taha's view but are aspects today of sharia as derived from the Medinan texts of the Qur'an—the revelations of the transitional stage of humanity's embrace of Islam. Because the most important function of sharia courts in Sudan is in the area of family law, including issues regarding polygamy, dowry, and divorce, the Republicans had to be careful in changing the rules. Moving too far from sharia even today could render marriages invalid, leading to formal charges of fornication and leaving children illegitimate.

Nevertheless, in his writings Mahmoud Mohamed Taha emphasized the historical context of the Qur'an's revelations about polygamy, that it was not "an original precept in Islam," and that it conflicted with the goals of women's complete equality with men. In *Reform and Development of the Islamic Personal Law* he wrote about polygamy, "It is not acceptable!"[12] There were a few polygamous men, already married, in the formative years of the Republican Brotherhood, and they were welcomed on the grounds that it would be unjust to have them divorce their wives just to conform to Republican standards. There was also a seldom followed principle that taking a second wife was acceptable in cases of infertility, again calling divorce an unjust solution for the barren wife. Some have suggested the Qur'anic injunction that a man could take more than one wife as long as all wives were treated equally, to be in itself forbidding multiple wives in that everyone understands that it is absolutely impossible to treat two (or more!) women equally.

Muslim marriage as outlined in Islamic sharia is actually a very simple relationship of which dowry is a standard regulated component. As such, it was marked for elimination by Mahmoud Mohamed Taha's understanding of the Qur'an. "Islam's rejection, on principle, of the concept of dowry was based on the fact that the dowry represents the price of a woman at a time in history when women were taken in one of three ways: as spoils of war, by kidnapping, or by purchasing them. As such, the dowry is a mark of women's inherited insignificance that must be discontinued when women's dignity and integrity are realized through the implementation of Islam's original precept."[13] However, there was also a need to keep in conformity with sharia in Sudan so that Republican marriages were legal. Their dowry payment was thus "one Sudanese pound," a small sum thought to be equivalent to what the Prophet had offered as dowry in his day. Of course, as the dowry was greatly reduced, the woman did receive many rights in the marriage contract which were not necessarily a part of Sudanese convention. As frequently as the topic of marriage came up among the (single) brothers in my house, the suggestion of one brother pushing another to marriage by opening his wallet and offering to lend him a pound for the dowry came up as well.

Divorce was the final component of Republican guidelines for modern marriage. Taha wrote, "Islam's original precept is the continuity of the relationship between spouses. Thus, a man's wife is his corresponding part, the manifestation of his self outside himself. She is the totality of outward signs corresponding to the man's self."[14] But compassion and practicality reigned with the Republicans as well, and divorce was understood as giving people a "second chance" if the first marriage did not work out. Their point was that the wife would not suffer the stigma of "repudiation" and would have equal rights to divorce in Republican marriage. In other words, the Republicans held to the Prophet's hadith that said divorce was "the worst 'halal,'" that is, the most terrible of things acceptable to God.

The key elements of Republican marriage were summarized in an important booklet published by the organization in 1971, *Khutwat nahw ala zowaj fil islam* (A Step to Marriage in Islam). The notion of "steps" covered the obligations of sharia in force in Sudan, assuring that couples marrying under these rules would be compliant with Sudanese law. The points were included in a certificate that was the pullout of the booklet. It was taken to the marriage ceremony and signed by the parties to the marriage there. Marriage in Islam itself was seen by Mahmoud Mohamed Taha as the ultimate goal, the complete elimination of guardianship of man over woman. All of these rights, Taha said, would be realized when the Path of the Prophet is followed to the second message of Islam.

One of the ways in which the Republican movement was propagated was through Republican brothers marrying women who were not yet members of the organization but who became so through marriage and raised their children as such. Occasionally, Republican sisters would marry non-Republican men as well. And there were also frequent pairings from within the community, men and women having a chance to hear what each other had to say in one of the jelsa—meetings at the home of Ustadh Mahmoud—or witness each other's religiosity at a dhikir. Of course, both of these activities provided informal opportunities for chatting before and after so that people could get to know one another, opportunities that were fairly hard to come by otherwise. Many brothers and sisters told me how their lives in the brothers' or sisters' houses had prepared them for the cooperative aspects of marriage.

The Republican marriage ceremony showcased the movement's values and principles on the public stage. The prospective bride and groom first sought a meeting together with Ustadh Mahmoud to tell him of their intentions. With his blessing he would urge that the wedding ceremony be scheduled within a few weeks of their meeting with him and would also announce the engagement at a jelsa the same day. The verse of the Qur'an that says, *Keep themselves chaste, until God gives them means* (24:33) would seem to dictate the rapidity of the process from engagement to wedding. And in that there was not a large dowry to save for there seemed to be no other reason to delay the ceremony. It was the selection process—whom shall I marry?—that often delayed marriage more than anything else. And this was always a major topic of discussion over lunch in the brothers' houses.

Republican ceremonies for the life cycle, weddings, funerals, and infant naming (*simaya*)—all had the same basic outline in keeping with the Republican de-emphasis on ritual. Men and women shared responsibilities in all of these ceremonies; there were no special ceremonies reserved for men or women. The Republican ideological foundation for this principle was that women were excluded and secluded when their knowledge and intelligence were not as developed as men's. Now women are men's equals and all activities are open to them. Reading of Qur'an in the Republican style, singing of spiritual poetry, *inshad erfani,* and light refreshments were presented at all of these ceremonies. No animals were slaughtered at these events, counter to Sudanese tradition. The nonviolent/socialist/vegetarian elements of Republican thought came together in the idea that the Prophet had engaged in animal (goat, sheep, camel) sacrifice that sufficed for eternity and for all of humankind. Republican children when asked by their young friends if they had had a sheep sacrificed at their house over this or that religious holiday could be heard saying with pride, "I am Republican; the Prophet sacrificed for me."

The wedding was the most public and important of all Republican ceremonies in that it involved the signing of a contract of equality between husband and wife, extending Republican spiritual authority further into the community. At the home of the host, usually the bride's family but sometimes the groom's or some other family member's if one or another branch was

A Women's Movement

opposed to Republican-style weddings, the *siwan* decorated canvas screens that are ubiquitous to urban Egyptian and Sudanese street celebrations, would be rented along with chairs and erected in the street outside the family house. These screens represented the tents that were parts of everyone's distant past. Police permission was sought for the day's disruption of traffic by the erection of the street-blocking screens. Many marriage contracts in Sudan actually take place inside mosques, often after the Friday congregational prayer. But in that Ustadh Mahmoud was regularly denounced from the pulpits of mosques, and that only men could attend the contract signing in the mosque, the setting of the family home was much more appropriate—and it was another opportunity for a public showcase!

The urban wedding party in Sudan outside of Republican circles had become a very expensive and noisy affair featuring a required "cocktail" meal of snacks and a big-name singer and band for a party that often lasted until dawn. The Republicans kept the focus on the spiritual elements of the ceremony, eliminating all of these trappings except for light refreshments served to the guests as they arrived, an hour or so before the time of the sunset prayer. Glasses of fresh lemonade were passed around as well as a tray of dates as symbols of Sudanese hospitality.

The bride and groom themselves actually had very small roles in the wedding ceremony. Wedding ceremonies in Islam are essentially signings of a contract binding the two families. Guests were seated with men on one side and women on the other—more out of convention than any strict segregation. It was important that as many Republicans as possible attend in order to show support for the couple and because in many cases family attendance might be low due to opposition to the Republican ideology or form of marriage. Brothers who had developed the art of Qur'anic reading in the lyrical Republican style—generally a crowd pleaser—started the event off. Then, the *mazoun,* the person from the Republican leadership who would actually perform the ceremony, would call the event to order and read from the document that the representatives of the two families would sign. This was usually preceded by a Republican leader in attendance explaining the process to the guests. Representatives/witnesses were usually fathers or some other senior male relative, signing the document that provided details on Republican marriage, including the wife's rights to divorce and that the husband would not take another wife. Then the symbolic dowry, one Sudanese pound, was given by the groom's representative to that of the bride. The *Fatiha*, the opening chapter of the Qur'an was communally read, hands were shaken and then there might be several odes sung from the Republican repertoire of Sufi-derived poetry. The ceremony concluded with taking down the canvas screens and using them as giant prayer mats for the communal sunset prayer. The newlyweds then set out on their new life together without new clothes or fancy honeymoon. In fact, I heard many stories or witnessed myself how on their first evenings together new couples would immediately go out and sell prodigious numbers of the Republican publications on the nightly book-selling campaigns. A post-wedding trip often included visits to Wad Medani to see senior Republican leader Ustadh Said el-Tayib Sha'ib and/or to Rufa'a to see Ustadh Khalid El Haj and the large numbers of brothers and sisters who lived in those two towns and who might not have had a chance to attend the wedding.

It was common to share impressions of the wedding at that evening's jelsa at the home of Ustadh Mahmoud. It was frequently reported by brothers or sisters sharing impressions at the meeting that the non-Republican guests marveled at the simplicity, efficiency, and spirituality of the ceremony, which was in stark contrast to the loud neighborhood block parties characteristic of urban weddings in Sudan. So the public Republican wedding was also good public relations for the movement. A well-known story from the era when I was an active witness to these weddings was that a non-Republican woman told a brother that she was very impressed with the wedding because during it even the "Christians [she was referring to me] read the *Fatiha*."

The largely middle-class phenomenon of Republican marriage was in many ways a response to the hyperinflation that had affected weddings and dowries in Sudan. The oil boom in the Gulf countries from the mid-1970s onward fueled tremendous demand for workers of all types in those countries, with small internal labor markets to supply the demand. These countries looked to the poorer Arabic-speaking countries (Morocco, Jordan, Palestine, Egypt, Yemen, and Sudan) to staff schools, banks, radio and television stations, airlines, hotels, and even working-class occupations such as in the huge irrigated farming schemes being set up to feed the newly wealthy Gulf residents. With the opportunity to make a significant amount of money in five or six years of employment in the Gulf, the price of a bride in Sudan rose substantially, often to the equivalent of $15,000 or more, which often did not include the expected suitcases full of clothing, taubs, gold jewelry, and household goods. Sudan government policy over the past twenty-five years has responded cynically to this opportunity, creating new programs of study in universities and technical colleges like medical technology or computer studies and encouraging the graduates to migrate to the Gulf for the badly needed remittances instead of using their skills to develop Sudan.

Ustadh Mahmoud's niece, Batoul Mukhtar, who had led the Republican sisters during the active years of the movement, took the radical step of going beyond the "steps to marriage in Islam" by considering herself "married in Islam" through a ceremony she described in her own words in a 1989 newspaper article:

> A few days ago in Khartoum North, a revolutionary
> marriage took place between Mr. Imad El Din Ali Idris
> of the Ministry of Agriculture and Natural Resources and

Miss Batoul Mukhtar Mohamed Taha of the Graduate College, University of Khartoum. The peculiar aspect of this marriage established on the original thought of Ustadh Mahmoud Mohamed Taha was conducted with respect to complete equality of rights and duties between the couple. The contract which divests guardianship of the other also permits the respective [member of the] couple to execute divorce at their initiative with each partner having the right to the moral provisions of the wedding contract. The new requisite precautions and disciplines are not exempted from the force of law.

Batoul went on to describe how the marriage took place simply between her husband and herself, with no dowry, no guardians present, and with guarantees for the wife of equality in every aspect of the marriage. She said that there was no dowry because "no man could put a price on a woman."

Batoul Mukhtar here demonstrates the mission orientation of the Republicans, always conscious of example and seeking didactic ways to communicate those lessons to the wider society. Her writing and sending the radical "wedding announcement" to a newspaper, a liberal one that would publish such a piece, was characteristic of Republican pride in the event-quality of their activities. It was also characteristic of Batoul Mukhtar's leadership style. As a leader of the organization, deputized by Ustadh Mahmoud in a sense, she made an important point of implementing all of the rights suggested in *The Second Message of Islam*. Gender segregation was not an "original precept" of Islam, as Mahmoud Mohamed Taha wrote, and Batoul led the way in gender integration. She was always forthright in starting conversations with men, pointing out to Republican brothers that they should be doing this or that, or speaking up about where the movement should be headed; I am sure she also corrected my Arabic a number of times—all while conducting herself with dignity. The other sisters followed her example in varying degrees and the cumulative impact was social change.

Batoul's leadership illustrates the limitless possibility contained in Mahmoud Mohamed Taha's postcolonial spiritual development thinking. Her act of "marriage in Islam" was a controversial one, causing her to be labeled elsewhere in the Khartoum press as having "joined her uncle in his apostasy" or as now "living in sin" with her husband in that no dowry had been exchanged. Batoul's marriage came at a difficult time for the Republicans, just four years after the execution of their teacher and two months prior to the coming to power of a Muslim Brotherhood–dominated military regime. Batoul Mukhtar's step was also bold in that the Republican Brotherhood had not engaged in public activities since the execution. But she had been a Republican all her life and was not going to back away from what she perceived to be steps in her own human development. She challenged her society to look carefully at what she perceived was possible for women.

The Republican sisters participated in creating and building institutions in which they could see themselves and in which they could thrive. These were not institutions established exclusively for women but rather were developed in consideration of women as part of the *ummah*, the Muslim community that confronted a modern world. The experience of the Republican sisters raises the possibility of religiosity as a sustainable foundation for development. The Republicans understood that spiritual links to education opened the mind and soul simultaneously and powerfully, an opening that was hard to close. This was religiosity with a built-in orientation toward progress, tying social change to advancing spiritual knowledge, one carefully applied to the other. The sisters learned what knowledge and skills were needed to fully participate in a very dynamic community, a community facing challenges to its very existence. The organization learned from the sisters and learned how to put that knowledge and those skills to use to everyone's betterment. The sisters felt confident to take on the challenges of al-duniya, (the material world) provisioned with a methodology that lead to inner peace and security in their identity as Muslims, and an articulate perspective on their rights. They spoke frequently of how their work outside of the movement with colleagues in schools, nongovernmental organizations, and in government service heightened their identity as Republicans because they could now see the integrity in their own practice of Islam. The greatest *dawa* or mission that the sisters served was to conduct themselves as modern Muslim women in these professional settings. If much was to be taken from the sisters in that regard, much was given as well by their association with the Republican Brotherhood in terms of dignity, self-respect, equality, and the promise of freedom.

5
Communicating Islamic Reform

Small Media, Big Ideas

O n the east bank of the Blue Nile is the village of Hilaliya, not far from the region in which Ustadh Mahmoud was raised. We visited the tomb of a holy man there, a wali, who was celebrated for the miracles he performed that attracted followers to his *maseed,* a Sufi school for Qur'an study. We saw the site of his best-known miracle, the *ghar,* an underground cell, which he constructed for his long periods of fasting and contemplation of God. To get to this underground cell is a feat unto itself. You crawl through a hole in the dirt floor of a room above the cell, and then descend down a rickety steep and narrow staircase. In an act that I suppose could be called "Sufi tourism," we climbed down into the cell and listened to one of the disciples of this wali's tariqa explain that he was able to endure longer and longer passages of time in the cell, eventually reaching ninety days, without food or water—nothing but God. While I might have referred to this visit facetiously as "Sufi tourism," neither Ustadh Mahmoud nor his followers would have used that term. The intention of our visit was not to "enjoy ourselves" but rather to appreciate the intense spirituality of men who lived close to God in this region in the past.

When we climbed down the staircase to the cell we found a simple angareb rope bed, where the holy man would lie during his periods of seclusion. There was also a tube to provide air from the upper reaches of the building to the cell, through which the holy man could breathe. The performance of miracles like this attracted adherents to the maseed in Hilaliya and came at a time of nineteenth-century Islamic revival in Sudan—and the great competition for the souls of Sudanese.

Everything else about this phenomenon we left to *Allah aa'lim*, "God knows best." The Republican perspective on these exploits of the Sufis was that the old Sufis' focus was far more on the actions of devotion than on ideas. My own view of the practices of these old Sufis was that their efforts to recruit followers in this manner were the origins of Sufi method, an exuberant or rigorous illustration of a path to God's knowledge. But Khalid El Haj told me on that visit to Hilaliya, "These were static views of ibada, what one had to do in the performance of religious duties, rather than on making progress in the performance of that ibada." Nevertheless, other Republicans on our group visit to Hilaliya that day voiced the view that the approach of these old Sufis was *basic* to the development of Republican thought. The intensity of prayer, the strict focus on God, the attention to one's practice of Islam, were all components of what became the Republican idea. "These were our roots," one brother told me, indicating why Republicans—for the most part—demonstrated respect for the *awlia,* the holy men of the past. But many also dismissed this kind of Sufi activity as dhikir bidun fikr ("remembering God without much reflection"). Some viewed this activity as an indication of how the Republicans understood that their contemporary practice of Islam and their following of the path of Prophet was in fact in continuity with the Islam around them rather than a break with it. There was great need of reform, as they pointed out without rest in their talks, lectures, books, and discussions, but it was still all about getting as close to God as possible.

But there were other currents—knowledge of the actions of Mahmoud Mohamed Taha—which led Republicans to believe they were in the presence of a man who had progressed far down the Path of the Prophet. For the most part, these were narratives reported in very respectful tones by Republicans, almost always concerning Ustadh Mahmoud's intense spirituality, not an aspect of his everyday interaction with his followers. And these narratives were generally being reported second- or thirdhand in that few were witnesses to this level of Ustadh Mahmoud's spirituality—his followers believed in that spirituality. Osman Bashir Malik said to me, "If you see something, tell us all," in reference to observations such as these, or dreams, mystical visions that one might have. Although Ustadh Mahmoud did not want these events to be the public focus of his work, the brothers and sisters were accumulating overwhelming evidence that they were being guided along the right path. Osman's own vision that he was telling me about was observing a light emanating from around the brothers' and sisters' feet during a session of dhikir (chanting) at the home of Ustadh Mahmoud.

Brother Hashim told me a story over a winter breakfast in Omdurman, on one of my visits to Sudan in the last few years. Hashim, who was trained as an English teacher, said that one morning he was selling Republican books in one of the hospitals in Omdurman. He went from ward to ward primarily focusing on book sales to friends and family members visiting patients. He came across a man very sick from cancer lying in a bed, and spoke to him, realizing that he knew him. "Aren't you so-and-so of the Republican Brotherhood?" Hashim asked. "Yes, I am," the patient replied. It was odd to find any Sudanese alone in a hospital, particularly a Republican. Visiting the sick was a major social duty of everyone; not to mention that visitors always provided the badly needed supplements to the food served by the hospital. But Hashim raced back to the home of Ustadh Mahmoud to report what he had learned. When he told Ustadh, the latter was elated and replied, "God bless you! You found him!!" And the clear implication was that Ustadh Mahmoud knew all about the brother in the hospital but kept his own counsel and directed the brothers in other spiritual ways, particularly brothers and sisters whom he felt were receptive to this form of communication. That it was Hashim who found the sick man was significant. Some would say that this was Hashim's reward for his attention to praying deeply, for "getting inside prayer." He had made solid progress along the path of the Prophet and therefore his knowledge of God was strengthened.

These internal forms of communication, between Ustadh Mahmoud and his followers, were not something that would be relayed to the wider public as characterizing the Republican view of Islam. This was an element of the contradiction, the tension between the deeply mystical roots of the brotherhood and the democratic/socialist/observant Muslim face of the organization that everyone wished to convey to the wider society. The Republican Brotherhood was in reality both of these aspects, which is why in their efforts to communicate who they were to a wider Sudan, their point was always that "my effort in conveying this message is primarily about deepening my own understanding of it." On my part, I did not know how to react to stories like the one of Hashim above. I tried hard to appreciate them from the perspective of a believer working on his faith. However, I did arch an eyebrow when told the story of an elderly senior brother, Hassan Hijaz, who was devoted to his teacher, Ustadh Mahmoud, and to the weekly chanting at his house. Hassan was running late and could not find a taxi to get him to the pre-sunset dhikir, yet nevertheless appeared there just in time for the start of the chanting.

This kind of memory of Ustadh Mahmoud and the aura around him was very common and frequently shared among the brothers and sisters, reinforcing the idea that they had experienced a unique human being. These accounts were not secrets, but some of the brothers were very sensitive to the idea that their approach would be dismissed as nothing more than Sufi mysticism if the focus had been on these events. The collective Brotherhood was working hard to represent a "modern" view of Islam, an "Islam for today," as some styled it. An example of the Brotherhood's concern was the tale spread, not by them, but by the Khartoum rumor-mill during the 1983–85 crackdown on the Republicans. It was reported that the reason why President Nimeiry had imprisoned Ustadh Mahmoud and virtually all of the leadership was that Nimeiry feared that if Ustadh Mahmoud ordered it, his followers would burn Khartoum to the ground.

Mystical knowledge was a component of Sufi Islam, and it characterized the faith wherever it spread on the African continent. It contrasted with a legalistic or theological approach to Islam, and it could be associated with charlatans as well. The sensitivity about mysticism arose from the notion of shirik, which could be translated as "idolatry." One of the most fundamental precepts in Islam is that there is no person or amulet or spirit between the believing Muslim and God; the believing Muslim did not need anyone or anything to intercede on his or her behalf with God. The Sufis would talk about how their odes, their visits to the awlia, or other esoteric practices demonstrated respect for those who seemed to have understood how best to worship God. It was a way to learn their methods of approaching God. And the "anti-Sufi" Islamic revivals, like Wahabism that arose in nineteenth-century Arabia to wipe out this type of practice in Islam, were adamant in a strict, and eventually state-enforced in some cases, conviction that practices of Sufism could constitute the sin of shirik.

As the Brotherhood organized itself to present its message to the world, it could be said that the music, hymns composed by some of the brothers and odes from well-known Sufi teachers, constituted the transitional aspect of Republican communication. The hymns were an essential element of every Republican gathering, large and small, and in that most of the hymns had a chorus, everyone had an opportunity to participate in them, including me. I remember listening to tapes of Republican music, what they called inshad, while driving with Abdullahi An-Na'im, and he remarked how he could tell if the tape was made while Ustadh Mahmoud was part of the group or not. Ustadh did not sing during these sessions, but his presence inspired everyone to their strongest voice.

Songs for Waiting

The qaseeda (ode) was a key representation of Republican values and ideas, expressed in a beloved Sudanese cultural form. I was always impressed with the many ways that form could be interpreted. An ode written in the early 1980s, as the movement moved toward its major confrontation with the regime of President Jaafar Nimeiry, entitled *a-Dinu Humu* ("They Are Religion") articulated the group's beliefs in a popular way. *A-Dinu Humu* was a somber ode, sung initially by some of the best *munshidiin* in the organization; it featured strong lyrics and soaring vocals. Sometimes an evening jelsa would go so long as to prompt the leaders to provide asha, supper, for the brothers and sisters, rather than making them wait to reach home for this meal. On these occasions a team would be formed quickly in the midst of the meeting and excused to go out and purchase bread, foul, and salads, in order to make vegetarian sandwiches to feed the large crowd.

My friends got me appointed to this team, knowing that I would probably enjoy making sandwiches more than snoozing at the meeting. The work required an assembly line at one of the nearby brothers' houses for such a large order (sandwiches for 100–200 brothers and sisters in attendance). As the bread was sliced and foul spooned onto the sandwich at this particular assembly line, a brother of fine voice broke into an upbeat rendition of the qaseeda, to everyone's delighted surprise. He introduced a new way of performing this ode—a tone and a beat from outside circles of Islam-inspired music—and thereby extended the life of the ode and its uses into more corners of the Republican experience. My friend's interpretation of the ode, which had become a Republican favorite in a short period of time, would never be performed in the presence of Ustadh Mahmoud or senior leadership and was strictly reserved for entertaining the brothers or sisters while at work, cleaning house, or performing other chores. But the words and message remained the same despite the "cool" rendition. Everyone liked to follow Ustadh Mahmoud's prescription of "*inshid* [sing] or listen to *inshad* all day long."

"*A-rakaa fi yanjelee hazanee,*" "When I see You my sadness goes away," is the refrain of a popular Republican qaseeda. Written by Isam El Boushi, an academic and prominent member from Wad Medani, the poem refers of course to God, but I also heard this poetry on the level of personal relations among this tightly knit social group. I was proud of myself for figuring out the meaning of the poetry, and used the line when again hosted by the brothers and sisters to a farewell function after a short recent visit to Sudan. As I closed my remarks, with thank-you's to the assembled group, I said that I would come back to Sudan because *a-rakaa fi yanjelee hazanee* (see translation above!), and all the sisters at the gathering collectively sighed, "awhhhhh."

For the members of the Republican Brotherhood, music was a distinctive part of both the movement's character and its image in the wider society. Music moved across a continuum of social construction around the rituals associated with prayer and around public culture through the appreciation of song and strong voices. And music communicated the Brotherhood's message of progressive change in Islam both through the mystical meanings of the lyrics, and in the person of the musicians themselves, particularly the women who courageously sang out in public. The picture of a Republican Sister leading a chorus of men and women in a public place endures for me as the strongest evidence that the philosophy embodied by this movement was liberatory for women.

The music represented multiple dimensions of the movement, but its most important element was its relation to daily spiritual renewal. Republicans used music for recruitment, religious study, that is, prayer or ibada, community-binding ritual, attracting brothers and sisters to meetings, inspiration, and fruitful expenditure of time. Music has some degree of controversy in Islam; for example, the more conservative Islamic thinkers see it as noncanonical, that is, not prescribed in Muslim ibada or the routine of prayer. The call to prayer, adhan, is distinctly sung by the muezzin, and there are many forms of Qur'anic recitation that have a melodic quality. But nevertheless, in the Republican context as taught by Mahmoud Mohammed Taha, the singing of spiritual poetry contributed greatly to wider community appreciation of the Republican interpretation of Islam. Inshad was seen as a cultural product of the quest for the hidden, while the music remained subordinate to the spiritual text. Performance of Republican qasaid is a method to reveal that which is hidden, a binding ritual, which also demonstrates the *Sudan-ness* of Republican thought. Words by the Sufi philosopher An-Nablusi found in a Republican qaseeda, echo this point, "Music is the building that may reveal the hidden."

The Republican brothers and sisters would call for music at any of their gatherings, most particularly if there was a munshid present. The singing of inshad emerged from the group's custom of having guests at their meetings who would perform *medeh,* traditional Sudanese Sufi odes to God and/or His Prophet, Mohammed. Meetings would be adjourned with these hymns, and eventually Republicans themselves began to use the poetry of historic Sufi figures, like Abdel Gadir al-Jailani, An-Nablusi ,or Ibn Arabi, set to contemporary music written as a Republican Brothers contribution to the art form.

Every type of singing ability was welcomed, encouraged, and supported. My Republican research assistant, Shams, told me the story of how he had come upon Ustadh Mahmoud repairing the seat of a plastic chair in his house. Ustadh Mahmoud's followers were deeply committed to serving their teacher, so this young brother quickly proposed that he complete the chair repair for Ustadh Mahmoud. Shams told me that Ustadh Mahmoud said to him, "You work on becoming a good munshid (singer), and I will repair this chair." Inshad was the largest cultural output of the Brotherhood and the most widely shared. One brother told me, "We get to know each other through singing—we know the strong voices, the funny voices ('so and so is always off-key' or 'he has no rhythm'), and we comment on these voices—informally. We are united as a chorus; I have shared a favorite qaseeda with you, and now we have one more aspect of our lives together as brothers." Such discussions or analysis were never officially sanctioned, that is, singers were not "rated," because the emphasis was on everyone participating.

I was talking with a young brother, Mahmoud Sharif, who had a beautiful voice and was a popular munshid. His popularity extended to singing gigs at non-Republican weddings all over the region. He told me that there were "basic" or even "official" munshidiin. I poked him a bit about this, and he showed embarrassment because of the apparent lack of modesty in his statement. But modesty may be hard to come by—a real burden—because the good singers were built up so as leaders of the organization, and they were representatives of, in part, the Republican approach to a public Islam. While there was great tolerance for all voices heard at a singing meeting, there was great excitement for the best voices because these voices were so important in representing the community to the wider world, an element of intense pride. Community commentary on the singing was generally limited to (1) the sources and meaning of the odes, or (2) the singers' length of time in service and the development of their skills. The munshidiin were in great demand for events like weddings and important meetings, or even if a brother had invited a large group for breakfast or lunch to his house, he might make sure that a good munshid was on the guest list as well.

Although participation in the singing may be paramount, comprehension of the poetry and putting that meaning into practice comes next in importance. The odes held great meaning for the movement. They were a comprehensive, culturally based instrument of devotion, an aspect of prayer. The issue of prayer was central to Republican thinking, and inshad was an extension of the complete dedication to the act of prayer. Prayer in the Republican spiritual methodology was not simply the rote recitation of ancient texts but was the word of God intended for our comprehension. The objective was to move *inside* the meaning of prayer as one prayed. And inshad provided an important and social opportunity to interrogate the meaning of prayer— one could pose questions about the sense of a particular word or formulation in the poem. This was very different from the act of praying itself in that prayer was a solitary act that by custom went uninterrupted. The lyrics to an inshad piece are repeated by a chorus, a learning process for many in that they may be exposed to Islamic "technical terms" from the spiritual realm for the first time in a qaseeda. But the words are also repeated because we love to hear them; they are beautiful and deeply meaningful.

At an early morning jelsa (meeting) that I attended at the home of Mahmoud Mohammed Taha in Omdurman, the brothers and sisters were singing a favorite hymn that contrasted the concepts of "being" and "becoming" (*kun fayakuun,* the difference was about stasis versus progress). Ustadh Mahmoud stopped the hymn in the middle of the piece and posed the question: "Who can tell me the difference between these two concepts?" he asked. Silence hung in the room until one of the brothers offered an answer. "*La,*" no, responded Ustadh Mahmoud. "Who else has an answer?" The interrogation continued for a minute or so until one brother provided an answer that satisfied Ustadh Mahmoud. He elaborated a bit, and then the brothers and sisters continued with the hymn. An important theological lesson had been taught, in the context of an activity that the students of Ustadh Mahmoud all enjoyed.

These early morning meetings were a part of an intense program of activity that filled the days and nights of the members of the Republican Brotherhood. Song cast away *ghafla* (neglect of religious duty, thoughtlessness, or inattentiveness) and developed knowledge, deep knowledge—of the philosophical details of the Republican ideology and of the multiple dimensions of God, as revealed by the Sufi poets. A brother described for me a morning meeting at Ustadh Mahmoud's home in 1977 in which a qaseeda was being sung that moved Taha deeply. He told the assembled brothers and sisters that he felt a strong spiritual presence had descended upon the group because of the intensity of their devotion through song. Mahmoud then told the brothers and sisters to come and get their share of this baraka. So everyone in the room filed out shaking Ustadh Mahmoud's hand as they left, which was how they took their share of this blessing.

Such a way to start the day! Inshad was what completed the movement. It was a vital component and an emblem. It was the articulation at the highest socially expressed level of Republican values and beliefs. It ordered the Republican day. The poetry required thoughtful effort; it had to be *penetrated*. But it represented nonarticulated gifts as well, such as that of the angel visiting a Republican meeting. Ustadh Mahmoud used inshad as part of his sense of the binding force of ritual as he sent his followers off that morning knowing that all had shared in his vision of spiritual faith.

Improvisational skills and "style" characterize the work of the "official" munshidiin of the movement. The chorus is indulgent, going along wherever the lead singer will take them—usually. Sometimes the tune just does not jell with the chorus, perhaps a function of the singer not always ready to be called upon to sing by the leader of the meeting. And sometimes the chorus may run away with a song, taken in by the rhythmic chanting choruses that end most qasaid. A sort of tug-of-war may ensue where the lead singer, the munshid, is trying to wrap up the piece but the chorus is intent on participating to the fullest and enjoying the chanting. The leader almost always gives up in these cases and follows the chorus to whatever conclusion it wants.

The singers were certainly recruited by Ustadh Mahmoud, as described above in the story of the young man who was encouraged by him to sing. But there were other means to becoming a singer as well. A thirty-one-year-old munshid told me that he had sung as a Republican Brother for ten years. He had a dream in which Ustadh Said, an important leader of the organization and head of the group in Wad Medani, told him to sing while touching his back saying "sing, sing, sing." Many of the best singers came from family traditions of Sufi *medeh* and/or had even sung for other organizations or in popular Sudanese music, for example, for weddings. There is a still an opportunity for art—evidenced by the high praise for rich voices and the effort the strong munshid makes in improvisation and voice innovation. The training of the munshid may extend simply from listening to tapes of inshad over and over again, or through early exposure to medeh through association with a Sufi organization or khalwa at a young age. I have also seen singers in their spare time studying slips of paper with the lyrics written on them—perhaps scribbled by a brother who had already memorized the piece—because it is important that the words not be sung from a written text. With leading the chorus and paying attention to what the meeting's leader may want to do, it would be difficult to read the lyrics while singing in any case.

My friend Khalid Mohammed El Hassan told me that, while his family had been committed Republicans for some time, he essentially became a Republican singer in 1977. He stated that inshad "got me more involved with the movement, it was a successful means of dawa [Islamic mission]." Khalid has many stories of his experiences as a singer; his big voice was important in attracting people to meetings, particularly in public. He told me a story of a trip (wafd) to Kassala on the train with a delegation of thirty, including seven brothers who were leading singers of the group. While riding the train, the whole delegation had broken into such strong inshad that even the train conductor joined in the chorus. The singers of the organization had their own grouping within the brotherhood and where leadership was recognized based on knowledge of the group's purpose. At one point Ustadh Mahmoud told him, "When you sing alone you are free to raise your voice as high as you want, but when you sing with Abdalla Fadlalla (another important Republican singer) you don't have to raise your voice above him. He is your sheikh in inshad." Then Ustadh Mahmoud went on to tell them the story of a sheikh from the major Sufi center of Abu Haraz. This sheikh was short, and one of his followers was extremely tall. Ustadh Mahmoud said, "Whenever they appeared together, the follower always bent over because he had never wanted to appear in the eyes of the people taller than his sheikh."

Inshad was also instrumental as an element of Republican preparation for its public speaking platforms, its book distribution campaigns, readiness for journeys or for conflicts of a political nature, and at Republican baby naming and marriage ceremonies. But inshad also provides a time for reflection, which one could see in the faces of the singers. And as I recall a Republican brother greeting me on the phone with the sung line of a favorite qaseeda, the music was foremost a form of joyful communication. The meaning of inshad to members of the organization was clear. As Khalid told me, "My mastery of inshad provides clear evidence of my self-improvement, my movement down the path of tariq Mohamed—first I see that I learn more of the odes, second, that I improve my singing, and third, that I have better coordination of the chorus."

The Republican Brotherhood was characterized by a highly intellectual ideology—and song was one of the more pleasant,

146

accessible, and culturally-based means to absorb that ideology. A typical venue for singing would be the jelsa. I've reported scenes from many of them in this book. During the heartiest days of the movement, song would either be an introductory part of the meeting, or perhaps an informal meeting would be called specifically for the music. The meeting would be held at a leader's house, sitting on beds in the courtyard if the weather was warm, or huddled inside the largest room of the house if during the rains or cooler months.

The leader of the meeting would be seated in a chair, and other chairs would be squeezed among the beds brought out to serve as benches for younger members of the group. Older brothers and sisters would be seated in the chairs, and usually the singers would be assigned chairs as well, both out of respect and with the knowledge that the breath flows better in that position (although I have seen younger singers actually performing from a crouching position on a mat on the ground, positioned there under crowded meeting circumstances).

Children were included in these meetings. The smallest would be sleeping in mothers' laps or laid between two women seated on the beds. Other children may be sleeping through the meeting as well, and older children may actually participate by learning the songs. Indeed, something I observed on a recent trip to Sudan was the encouragement of younger children—as young as eight—to sing. The few that I encountered were in fact children of well-known Republican singers.

The chorus does not know which pieces will be chosen by the singers, and as the singer is designated by the meeting's leader, we see him or her take on a downward look of deep concentration, seeking *warid*, or direct communication with God, as the song emerges from his or her repertoire. The chorus tries to keep up with the munshid, the success of which depends on the familiarity of the group with the piece he or she has chosen. In some cases the lead singer may stumble with the words and is quickly assisted by a knowledgeable member of the chorus. There was, however, a long series of organized meetings in which recordings of the favorite munshidiin were made, complete with introductory commentary by one of the leaders of the movement. In these cases, the chorus did know which qaseeda would be next on the program.

Sometimes in Sudan the dhikir or spiritual songs are so intense one can imagine something holy descending upon the group. I was with a small group of brothers observing a particularly strong non-Republican *noba*, or Sufi drumming and chanting session, at a cold January midnight in Rufa'a, commemorating the death a year earlier of a prominent local sheikh. The experience provided an opportunity to compare Republican Brotherhood attitudes toward music with those of a more traditional Sufi group. About fifty men ranging in age from sixteen to seventy had gathered in the empty lot next to a walled compound. They had placed sticks (*asaya*) in the center of the circle, and the leaders of the group stood together at one end. This group consisted of a munshid or two and two men who played a small drum or a large *tabla*. The music for each medeh started slowly, and the lines sung by the munshid were repeated by the gathering. Off to the side on three sides of the circle, women and young children had gathered to watch. Some had brought food. As the beat of the music grew more intense, the Sufis increased their rhythmic motion. At one point the beat increased fourfold, and the brothers were swaying in time. A few were actually overcome by the intense beat and had to be assisted by others, usually to a place outside of the circle where they tried to calm down. These individuals always came back for more, however. Movement cannot be removed from the music. As with dhikir, there is an aspect of transcending the corporeal. And as with fasting, there is an aspect of endurance here.

I had joined this noba group—just to observe—with a few of my Republican brothers from Rufa'a. In fact we had been woken up by the noise in a house nearby and had come out to watch—we found that the beat infected us as well. And soon this stoic group of modern-thinking Muslim Republicans was swaying back and forth to the rhythm of the tambour. One of the brothers remarked to me that Mahmoud Mohammed Taha had not approved of such vigorous shaking in the practice of dhikir. "An empty drum makes the loudest noise," Mahmoud had said. The rhythm, however, is hard to resist, which may have been Ustadh Mahmoud's point. We talked about the dominant presence in the circle of young men—under the age of twenty-five—and decided that they had been attracted by the music and rhythm, there not being much else to do in this small eastern Gezira town.

The Republicans often compared their spiritual-cultural contributions to the type of conventional Sufi arts, the music and rhythms, demonstrated at this midnight gathering. Republican poetry, in contrast, was composed as an aspect of prayer, and the Republicans felt that dhikkir bidun fikr ("to remember without reflection," without thinking about what you were doing) was an empty exercise. Although early Republican thinking was that musical instruments should not compete with the human voice in inshad, the Republicans who are making new homes in the US community of Iowa City, Iowa, are experimenting with the organ and oud (lute) as accompaniment to inshad. They are also singing compositions by a well-known Sudanese popular singer, Al-Musali.

Music is *the* program for Republican Brotherhood meetings in this era, more than thirty years beyond the execution of Mahmoud Mohamed Taha. The opportunity to engage in this aspect of communal prayer is a major attraction of this era of nonpolitical meetings. The sheikh or meeting leader designates singers (1) to get a sense of their abilities, (2) for maximum participation of those willing to sing, and (3) to let everyone else hear what this person may have to offer. Newcomers to Republican thought—of whom there are still seen many in Khartoum—also can learn the songs in this way. And progress is being reported: al-Musali is writing down the music that accompanies Republican qasaid. This is a very new development emerging from the Republican laboratory that is Iowa City, perhaps lending a focus to the movement that avoids the theological/political discourse that got the movement in trouble in Sudan.

In a recent Khartoum conversation about the music that I had with a group of brothers, one had a negative reaction to the introduction of musical instruments to inshad. He talked about how the instruments reduced the participation of the chorus and how Ustadh Mahmoud had said that inshad was for participation, not an audience. Another brother mentioned that he liked the new music emerging from the movement; new meanings and knowledge were emerging from the lyrics that he had not considered previously.

The musical message of the Republican Brotherhood has been particularly emblematic of the group's position on equality for women. Gradually women came to dominate this characteristic aspect of the movement. Hajja Rhoda, mother of my friend Khalid, mentioned above, was the first Republican sister to sing inshad in public—at a book exhibit in the early 1980s. She was also matriarch of a large family in Rufa'a, and she would raise the whole neighborhood from sleep with her daily azan. For some of the young sisters today who are important participants in song, the music is in great part what initially attracted them to the organization. The eight-year-old girl with a very strong voice mentioned above is the future of the Republican voice. Her mother was a noted *munshida*, and her father accompanies her to these meetings looking on proudly as his daughter masters the words in formal Sufi Arabic.

Participation is key. Everyone joins in the chorus, no matter what their musical ability. Some do "show off." Some just reflect quietly. Some are absorbed in deep concentration during qasaid, which sometimes is related to the particular atmosphere,

150

for example, if there has been a death or someone has said something profound at a meeting, or if there is a "mood." At the same time, it is common in religious music to have a chorus that everyone may follow, accommodating those—like myself—who might not know all the words to the poetry.

While participation is what drives the popularity of inshad as an aspect of Republican spiritual life, it is—to some extent—at odds with the cultural production aspects. I was with a group of brothers, mostly older men, having breakfast in a small Eastern Gezira town, Tamboul. Following the meal everyone urged the expert young munshid who was at the breakfast to lead the group in song. His voice was well known throughout the organization, and he was in high demand for his talents, sometimes compared to famous Sudanese singers. He and I had previously discussed the difficulty of performing when the chorus is weak, despite the high level of enthusiasm always in evidence. And he had told me, "Yes, a weak chorus may affect the mood of the munshid." As I listened to his strong voice and the relatively tired choral response to his soaring melodies, I was thinking I would have advised the young man to know his audiences better and select better-known pieces for groups that might not have the capacity to follow his newer musical style. But of course, he *did* know his group better than I: he asked to borrow my ever-present sociologist's pen when two of the brothers from the "chorus" asked that he write down the words to one of the qasaid that he had just sung. They wanted to learn it for the next time. The men had responded in a natural way to the daily imperative to make some progress on the Path of the Prophet.

Their collective point was that the beauty of the sung poetry motivated the Republican brothers and sisters to learn as much of it as they possibly could, and to use it for personal reflection. An aspect of prayer, it is a highly appropriate way to spend one's time on earth. "There are details of faith and of the Republican ideology in those verses, and I want to know as much as possible," some would say. "*Gowm*," community or group, is another term that appears frequently in the chorus lyrics of qasaid, again signaling the Republican theme of moving forward together in Islam.

Inshad is shared in a very natural atmosphere. For example, I attended one gathering in an extremely full house. Every room was taken up with people, including the two courtyards. And everyone was joining in the singing, although many could not see the leader of the meeting or the lead singers. A father who was sitting next to me was asked by the leader of the meeting to sing, and his two-year-old proceeded to climb into his lap while he did so, screaming that he wanted water ("*Baba, moya!*") while Dad was singing. No one moved to remove the child, an aspect of the early stages of Sudanese indulgent parenting, and the child's cries remained in the recorded versions of the jelsa. At the same meeting Suad Sulaiman, a well-known munshida, had just walked in the door late to the jelsa and taken a seat when the leader of the meeting asked her to sing. One of the brothers started to protest—half jokingly—in that she had not yet caught her breath, but she plunged into the piece with a taut look of pride on her face.

The Republicans are proud of the increasing impact their style of music is apparently having on both popular and Sufi music in Sudan, subtly and without fanfare. The major star El Kabali, has produced a record with Republican-influenced tunes. At the same time, the Republican music stands up remarkably well to globalization with no elements of Western music creeping into the production of new *gasaid*, except, perhaps inevitably, among the followers of Mahmoud Mohammed Taha living in the United States. The borders between the spiritual songs and those of al-duniya (this world) are sometimes difficult to discern. It was said that Mahmoud Mohammed Taha himself appreciated Mohamed Al Amin, a major Sudanese popular singer blind since birth, both for his rich voice and for his spiritual approach to overcoming his disability.

The Republican brothers and sisters living in exile in the United States have worked hard to continue the development of the organization. They were extremely excited when Ohio University's African Students Union designated the late Mahmoud Mohammed Taha as its African hero for the annual February celebration of African Heroes Day in 2001. Republicans in the United States pooled financial resources to bring to Athens, Ohio, a favorite munshida, Ikhlas Himet. Overcoming the financial and visa issues required a huge, concentrated effort, and a large contingent of Republicans descended on Athens that February for the event. Most of the US-based families had a cassette or several of her distinctive voice interpreting inshad. The visit of Ikhlas, to hear her voice live, was uplifting and stimulating for entire families and served as an important point of the group's continuing mission, and an important reason to see one another. The Republican community experienced a deep loss not long after Ikhlas returned to Sudan after her US visit, when she and her husband were killed in a car accident on the Khartoum-Medani road.

The *inshad erfani* (spiritual poetry) of the Republican Brotherhood was the finest and most accessible expression of the movement's clarity of vision, a vision of a world at peace. The human voice was the vehicle for this expression, practiced, spoken, recorded, and heard again and again as reminder and exhortation of what was possible for humankind on earth. My point in remembering these odes is to recognize the accomplishment of an Islamic grassroots organization composing such beautiful music and finding the voices to express it. Their work helped a sophisticated body of Islamic thought to sink into people's souls in a comforting cultural manner, and often eased the pain of longing for God and for country.

Reading Islamic Reform

The production of knowledge in the Republican Brotherhood continued with *hamla,* the campaign to discuss, write, publish, and distribute books about their spiritual ideas and commentary on the modern world all over Sudan. They were proud of managing to publish more than 200 titles and distribute about 1,000,000 copies of the books all over the country—primarily on foot. The Republicans and Mahmoud Mohamed Taha particularly had been banned from the nation's airwaves for their heretical views. Thus they put their energies into getting the books out there one way or another, in great part to help themselves plumb the depths of the Republican idea as deeply as possible. The production of texts was another element of the iterative process constructed by Mahmoud Mohamed Taha for his followers to improve their understanding of the Republican theology while becoming more articulate about it. It was another example for me of what stood out about this movement, about what made it modern and democratic.

Reading is fundamental in Islam. The word Qur'an itself comes from the root Arabic word for "reading." Sidewalks outside of mosques all over the world are crowded with sellers of texts and commentaries on the Qur'an, and bookfairs are important annual cultural events in many Arab cities. The Republicans joined this knowledge production, before email, YouTube, and PDFs, with a carefully constructed effort to get their ideas before the public. The iteration was between Ustadh Mahmoud and his followers, and between the followers and the wider society as it confronted some new thinking about Islam presented by terribly earnest Republicans. In all cases these Republican communication efforts were distinct from the commentaries available on mosque sidewalks and bookshops in that they were the product of the thinking of the entire Brotherhood and not of the learned *maulanas* and sheikhs who usually authored such tracts.

For me, the Republican book writing and public speaking campaign gave me more of the feeling that I was on the front line of social change, or rather, holding up the rear of that front line as best I could. Ustadh Mahmoud was, of course, an author of ten books, including the movement's manifesto, *The Second Message of Islam*. By the time I was on the ground in Omdurman, he had turned over the responsibilities of communicating the messages to his followers. This was both an exercise of his philosophy of guiding his disciples to activities that would improve their understanding of the Republican idea and in response to his harassment by the Sudan government. The energetic discourse of the movement generated ideas, themes, topics, and debates that found their way into the books. The morning meetings at the brothers' houses were important sources of ideas, and they were often carried through the evening discussions at the home of Ustadh Mahmoud. If an idea was thought to have potential for a Republican text, a committee would be formed to look for the way forward: Does this topic need more research or more exposure to the public on the streets? Or do we need to think about it more internally? I remember being called on to contribute to the development of Republican thinking on "democracy," because of assumptions about my experience as an American witness to it. I was asked to make the rounds to all of the brothers' houses for the early morning meetings as they opened an investigation of democracy. But whatever I had to say on the subject was certainly not accepted as the last word from the "expert." Rather, I was challenged repeatedly at that early hour over what brothers had read about poverty or racism in the United States or the obstacles to everyone sharing in democracy's fruits. The tract that emerged from this debate was forceful and direct, and, in essence, the perspective of the entire brotherhood. The final outline of the book in fact emerged very much in a democratic space, as the Republicans debated it at their outdoor evening meeting in the empty lot next to Ustadh Mahmoud's house.

The production of a Republican book titled *Al-Takamal* (Integration), about the 1982 decision of the governments of Sudan and Egypt to form a unified republic, a political scheme of Presidents Mubarak and Nimeiry, is an example of the group responding to the issues of the day in their writings. Republican opposition to political and economic integration with Egypt was based on their sense of Sudan's cultural and moral traditions, and on the fact that they felt Sudan unready for integration with another state when it had yet to achieve internal integration with its own South. This, of course, was also the issue that had launched Ustadh Mahmoud's pre-independence political career: his pursuit of the establishment of a Republic of Sudan instead of unity with Egypt or some sort of Islamic Khalifate under the Mahdi family. Another example of the topical interests of the movement was the series dedicated to International Women's Year in 1975. Some of their best sellers included a book on the prayers and practices of Islamic burial, traditions that the Republicans felt were being lost in contemporary society, and the book that described their own unique, efficient, and economical guide to Republican marriage. These books, which could be thought of as tracts or long pamphlets in many cases, reflected a refreshing concern for real-life issues rather than the esoteric topics of many religious publications of the time.

The process of the jelsa, or group meeting, leading to the production of a text was referred to in English by one of the movement's leaders as "brainstorming." When I asked what term he would have used in Arabic to describe this process, he offered *waridat* (from the Sufi term "warid" which is a direct communication from God). In a sense, he was using the metaphor of the group meeting at prayer, where each is communicating with God, to describe the process of thinking about ideas for the books. An illustration of how the group participated in composing these books is found in an incident where Ustaz Mahmoud was discussing the contents of a book that he was writing, "Learning How to Pray." An aspect of the text concerned the ablutions that immediately precede prayer. Taha stated that one thinks carefully about what you have done with that part of the body as you apply water to it to cleanse it. One of the brothers then contributed, "so it is like a *jelsa nafsiyan* [i.e., a private meeting between yourself and God]." Ustadh Mahmoud excitedly said, yes, that was the perfect term for the process, which was then incorporated into one of his book's chapter titles.

A finished manuscript was, in the early days of Republican publishing, the late 1960s and early 1970s, then carefully handwritten on duplicating material. Later, the book topics became so long that production moved to typing to save space and paper. Again, vigilant attention to error was essential because the duplicating sheets were so difficult to correct. The pages were then run off on a duplicating machine, essentially mimeographed, and then bound with a heavier paper cover. An artistic brother with beautiful handwriting would use classic Arabic calligraphy for the cover. Ustadh Mahmoud said, "The essence of art is freedom." The whole production process engaged the Brotherhood with elements of the wider society in that contracts for paper purchases in bulk and other supplies had to be negotiated with Khartoum merchants. A comical/sad incident occurred during the 1983 Nimeiry government crackdown on the Republicans when my typewriter was confiscated by the security police as the possible source of Republican books, despite the fact that my little plastic Remington portable only typed in the Roman alphabet, not Arabic.

The finished books were then ready for sale on the streets. The Republicans became their own distributors in this process and saw the "selling campaign" as a vital extension of their discussions in meetings among themselves. In fact, the campaign process was praxis or an application of the Republican's religious ideology in that it strengthened the individual's understanding of and commitment to that message. Over the years of their publishing program more than 200 titles were produced by the Republican Brothers. When a new book was ready for distribution, brothers and sisters would gather at the home of Ustadh

Mahmoud and prepare for the launch. I participated in a launch once, entrusted with carrying a package of a new book to the brothers in Rufa'a, *Hatha Hou a Sadiq el Mahdi* (This is Sadiq el Mahdi, a tract on the sectarian political career of the once and future prime minister of Sudan). As I left the house of Ustadh Mahmoud, he shook my hand firmly and whispered in my ear, "*Selem ala Sheikh Taha,*" ("Greet Sheikh Taha for me!"). Sheikh Taha, no close relation to Ustadh Mahmoud, was the holy man buried in the tomb in Rufa'a's old cemetery; Ustadh knew that I enjoyed visits to the awlia.

Often a session of prayer and reflection would precede the deployment of bookselling teams to the streets. It was important that members of the organization participating in the sale of Republican books be spiritually and intellectually informed of their contents. The bookselling campaign was seen as a test of one's mettle and of one's commitment to and knowledge of the Republican vision of Islam.

Fortified by prayer and hymn singing, the brothers and sisters set out for sales, usually in separate teams, except for husbands and wives. There were specific rules conveyed to me that were applied to those wishing to participate in the book distribution campaigns. The guidelines, which were largely common sense, included:

> You must be tolerant of others' viewpoints while selling the books.
>
> Do not talk with the public about issues you are not sure about.
>
> Make your first *hamla* (campaign) with someone more experienced than you are.
>
> Read the material before you attempt to sell it.
>
> Know the Qur'an because it is the foundation of all of our books.

Developing a high state of consciousness about what one was doing in the act of hamla (or any other act for that matter) was the purpose of discussing these rules with newcomers to the group.

The teams of brothers or sisters would generally head for the busy market areas across the Khartoum metropolitan area. It was not necessarily a hard sell, and sales were generally brisk. People were thirsty for information about their religion, particularly after the 1979 Islamic revolution in Iran. Sisters would stand on the street corner, offering the books by holding them fanned in their hands. Their white taubs stood out as advertising that the Republicans were around. The brothers might pursue sales a bit more assertively, asking passersby if they would be interested in learning more about the movement and its writings. It was common to see Republican books in the back windows of Khartoum taxis in that the cabdrivers were also looking for something to read while waiting for passengers.

Altercations did occur with opposing forces in the urban setting. I remember once going out on book sales with a group of four or five brothers. We were stopped by members of the conservative Wahabi group, which styled itself as strict followers of the Prophet Mohamed, right down to dressing as they imagined the Prophet Mohamed would. These guys started screaming at us, "Where are your beards??!!" in reference to their notion that an observant Muslim man should wear a beard as the Prophet did. The next morning I shaved off my mustache. There were also reports of sisters involved with book sales having their hair pulled or their collection of books thrown in the mud, by forces reacting to the "indecent" exposure of women selling books on the street. These incidents followed us to the United States as well. I hosted a lecture by Professor Abdullahi Ahmed An-Na'im at Ohio University, which featured a table where we were selling his translation of Ustadh Mahmoud's book, *The Second Message of Islam*. The table was left unattended during the talk, and we later discovered that a Saudi student had taken all of the books and thrown them in a trash can outside the hall. He later confessed and apologized to us.

Book sales by brothers in the small towns outside of Khartoum-Omdurman could be far more sedate and low key. A number of times I went with brothers on hamla in Rufa'a where we sold a book or two in the evening market and then stopped for Cokes at a small shop. After an hour or two of sales, wherever they took place, the teams would report back to the leadership in the evening meeting. As an important part of the meeting agenda at the home of Ustadh Mahmoud, book sales would be tallied with comparisons made of which books were the most popular. The price of each book was minimal, from five to ten Sudanese pounds. And the proceeds went into producing more books, with a brother with accounting skills keeping track of sales.

Another important part of the post-sale evening agenda would be discussing public reaction to the books. What was the public saying about our latest book or about us? "Impressions" fueled the meeting and often contributed to second or third editions of some of the books as their contents were modified based on some public reactions. These revisions usually revolved around clarifying a point of Republican thought that had been obscure in an earlier edition. The impressions segment could also be to discuss public reaction to Republican thought and be-havior in general because the organization was always extremely interested in how it was perceived and whether it was accepted. It could also be an opportunity for positive reinforcement as one brother described how another handled a difficult question from someone on the street. Ustadh Mahmoud focused intently on these "impressions" sessions and would often summarize them at the meetings.

The university campuses were also important venues for both book sales and for communicating the Republican message by other means. Wall newspapers were prepared carefully on rolls of white paper, perhaps 12 feet long by 4 feet high. Teams of brothers would usually transfer the contents of one of the latest Republican books to the paper by hand, with large lettering to highlight important sections or points. These would be taped up on bulletin boards provided by the universities for announcements by student organizations. Sometimes a brother or sister would be posted by the newspaper to answer questions, or sometimes brothers would spend the night guarding the newspaper from defacement by one of the other student religious groups opposed to Republican thought.

The Republicans would occasionally mount more ambitious exhibits of their books at the universities or elsewhere. A tent would be set up with tables inside covered with various editions of the Republican books. The sides of the tents would be decorated with colorful posters or banners that contained quotes from the books or from one of Ustadh Mahmoud's lectures. Several brothers and sisters would be available to take questions and supervise sales of the books. When one of the brothers referred to the opening of such an exhibit as an "inauguration," in English, I got myself in trouble by telling him that I thought that was too grandiose a term for the event. In my early days learning about the Republicans and their perspectives it was clear that I often missed the cues signaling the importance of all of these activities to those who organized and invested in them. The inauguration of the book exhibit actually did feature an opening lecture, singing of Republican hymns, and a good crowd of brothers and sisters, including those who were not university students. Eventually I grew to understand the strong unity that these group activities represented, and the intense pride people had in their successful launching.

Whether on the streets of Khartoum collecting impressions from the public about the Republican perspective or in a small town or on a delegation to a far corner of the country, I found these campaigns of the Republican Brotherhood to be part of Ustadh Mahmoud's genius in getting his followers to learn

Communicating Islamic Reform

about their country and its peoples on their own terms. There always was a strong sense of national purpose in the movement, certainly since its origins in the independence struggle. And the trips around the country that the Brotherhood sponsored, which they called wafd, "delegation," were low-key representations of their ideas, armed only with their simply produced books and their hymns. I had to adjust to traveling with them in Sufi style. The father of a brother died in the small Gezira village of Hilat Hammad. Ustadh Mahmoud assembled a group to represent the Republicans at the funeral. A couple of members of the delegation found me walking along the street in Omdurman and told me to come along on the journey. "I don't even have a toothbrush with me!" I complained. But I went with them to the village for a couple of nights where we sang Republican hymns at the wake-like event and learned about life in a very rural community. Someone bought me a toothbrush at a tiny shop in the village, and one of the farmers lent me a jellabiya to sleep in. We traveled *bidoon shunta* ("without a suitcase"), as my friend Khalid liked to call it.

This was the way to get to know a community and to demonstrate your level of commitment to understanding their life circumstances. You don't roll into town in a nice car and shiny shoes. You accept the bed that someone probably carried under his arm from his house to that of the family of the deceased; these sisal and wood beds were not that heavy. They get placed around outside, and the son of the man who carried the bed arrives with a thin mattress and a sheet and a pillow. You think about "effortless hospitality," but there *is* effort involved and you acknowledge it by being there. In the morning as you are getting ready to leave with the delegation, you accept the glass of sweet hot tea made with goat's milk from each of the pretty ceramic tea pots carried to the event by farmers from their wives' kitchens. Twenty glasses of goat-milky tea. And there is no way to say "no, thanks."

The most important, or dramatic rather, element of the Republican efforts to communicate their perspectives to the general public in the Khartoum area were the *arkaan* (singular *rukun*, meaning "corner" literally.) These talks held in public areas of the national capital were also referred to as a "platform" or *member* (the term also refers to the pulpit used by preachers in mosques and churches). The term "corner" came from one of the brothers who had studied in London and used to observe democracy in action at the Hyde Park Speakers' Corner. The Republicans were trying to assert their right to express themselves and share their views in a consistent manner, and in the absence of a right to appear on radio or in television broadcasts, they regularly scheduled these talks around town. The most famous and the most controversial speaker among the Republicans was Ahmed Dali, whom I described as a brothers' house leader in chapter 3. In fact this was Dali's job, and he was one of the only "employees" of the movement, as he was paid a small stipend to give talks on a daily basis.

Only brothers and sisters with the deepest understanding of the Qur'an and of the Republican ideology were permitted to represent the group in public in this manner. Ustadh Mahmoud would spend a great deal of time talking with these men and women about his ideas and about their knowledge of them, as well as strategies on how to present them in public. Most days Dali would meet early with Ustadh Mahmoud and then travel to the center of Khartoum to offer his rukun. He was a public intellectual in the tradition that sprang out of the Khartoum coffee houses in the 1920s and '30s, where men would gather to discuss the events of the day, presaging the independence era.

The established spot for Dali's event was under an enormous *aradeb* (tamarind) tree with large spreading branches that provided a great deal of shade in hot Khartoum. He also frequently spoke on the University of Khartoum campus. Dali's *rukun al-aradeba* attracted hundreds of people each morning. Some came out of intense support for the Republican idea; some were there to heckle or question every pronouncement; and many came just for the show. Some came to listen to Dali or other top-notch Republican speakers play with the language, another important part of the Republican rhetoric. Dali would stand in the shade of the tree with a chair that he might sit on or lean on as the morning went on. The crowd would form a large circle around him, enough to draw young girls selling peanuts or other seed snacks. Dali would begin with "Let us agree that . . ." and then his tone would often turn accusatory, pricking people's consciousness on issues such as women's equality in Islam. He frequently cited Qur'anic verses in support of what he was saying, and those with opposing views would also shout out contradictory verses. The devil may cite scripture for his purpose, Shakespeare said (in *The Merchant of Venice,* I believe). But this also pointed to the root of what Ustadh Mahmoud was trying to get at in his book, *The Second Message of Islam,* which explained the difference in revelations that came to the Prophet Mohamed in Mecca versus those revealed to him during the Medina phase of his Prophecy. The two phases often contradicted each other because, as Ustadh Mahmoud would explain, the Medina texts were revealed at a difficult time in the construction of Islamic society and were not meant for all time, as the Meccan texts were. Dali spent a great deal of time explaining this difference to his audience—with mixed results. He did not soft-pedal religion to his audience, like an American evangelist might do to the millions of Christians who tune into his US television broadcasts. He tried to speak at the level of the crowd, giving people, in his words, the "exact dose" of what he thought they could absorb.

The members of the Muslim Brotherhood targeted Dali in these talks, often planting members of the audience to challenge him or just heckle him. Part of this was due to Dali's own take-no-prisoners style of audience confrontation, telling his challengers that they were wrong without subtlety. Fist fights broke out occasionally as a result, and Dali was badly beaten by Muslim Brothers (often called by the Republicans, "MBs") at a University of Khartoum talk. He lost hearing in one of his ears that was never restored. Dali and the other Republican speakers took to the streets to denounce Muslim Brotherhood tactics and tendencies, the only voices in Sudan to do so.

Besides general ignorance of Islam's details and history, the greatest opposition to the Republican Brotherhood in Sudan was Sudan's branch of the Muslim Brotherhood. This group is best known today in the West as the party of Mohamed Morsi, the deposed president of Egypt. My own talks about the Republican Brotherhood in the United States have been met with some confusion, because of the association between "brotherhood" and "Muslim" in people's minds. Hassan al-Banna was an Egyptian schoolteacher who founded the Muslim Brotherhood in the 1920s. His early thinking about Islam was not radically different from Mahmoud Mohamed Taha's early ideas. They both railed against the colonial imposition of European values on Muslim peoples, and they both encouraged their followers to think more carefully as to how they were practicing Islam—particularly as an alternative to Western influence.

Where the two differed, or where their organizations diverged, was in the eventual adoption by the Muslim Brotherhood of violent means to make progress toward its political agenda. The Muslim Brotherhood has been an important (now banned) political party in Egypt and has been an extremely influential party in Sudan. The current regime governing Sudan took its essential philosophy from the Muslim Brotherhood and its guide in Sudan, Dr. Hassan al-Turabi (1932–2016). Al-Turabi was thought to have influenced President Nimeiry's decision to execute Mahmoud Mohamed Taha in 1985.

All of these talks, arkaan, lectures were thoroughly analyzed by the members of the Republican Brotherhood at their evening meetings with Ustadh Mahmoud. Other brothers and sisters went out on the speaking circuit around town, particularly on the university campuses, as they gained expertise and knowledge, and confidence from Ustadh Mahmoud that they understood the Republican idea thoroughly enough to stand up to the tough audience scrutiny of Khartoum. The brothers and sisters were *excited* by the reports of challenging debates taking place under the aradeba tree or elsewhere. They felt their cause moving forward even as they sensed their country falling behind in its understanding of Islam and what Muslims should do. As I listened to these talks in the streets and heard reports of people's impressions of them over and over again, I too felt increasingly transformed by Ustadh Mahmoud's pedagogy, with some help from the mystics. This was better than graduate school.

6
A Modern Muslim

Although the word "memoir" does contain the word "me," that etymological coincidence was not why I selected this form of narrative for my account of the Republican Brotherhood. Rather, I felt limited by academic approaches and—because literature on the Republicans was so sparse—I did not want to shoehorn my personal experience of this phenomenon into the meager literature on progressive social movements in the Muslim world. I was drawn to the inconclusiveness of a memoir because my experience is not the only story to be told of the Republican Brotherhood. I wanted to be free to share my observations about people whom I had grown to know well, while subjecting my observations to whatever authority I have mined in forty years of paying attention to Africa. Memoir also seemed appropriate in that so much of what the Republicans shared of Mahmoud Mohamed Taha and each other was recalled in the form of oral narratives, despite the highly literate state of the participants. Such reports were a comfortable way of remembering, common to the culture, and they could be quickly edited as one learned new details. The brothers and sisters were far more focused on their practice of faith than they were on collecting written stories.

With my decision to produce this memoir I am sure that I was also thinking it was time to get a personal account of this movement out there unencumbered by tentative frames. The memoir asserts the right, responsibility, and the privilege of witnessing that I hope in this case communicates the passion, vigor, and sincerity in which the Republicans approached belief. My intention has certainly been to contribute a book that promotes a nuanced understanding of how a Muslim society uses its faith to organize itself. Islam has become The Big Story in the West since the 1970s, but we've seen few changes in that story's core stereotypes over five decades.

As a human witness, I bear many flaws. I could not see everything. My Arabic was not *miya-fi-miya* (100 percent). I lacked a better half to witness the sisters' lives from the inside. But I asked many questions, including "What does that mean?" and tried hard to pay attention in a manner that indicated to all that I was willing to learn something new in Sudan, and report it. What I witnessed moved me and sometimes took my breath away.

Whatever my limitations, it was obvious to me that a secular civil society was not evolving in Muslim Sudan as may have been expected after decolonization. The dominant and complete presence of Islam in everyday life was a remarkable part of my education in Sudan. Every element of existence took place in an Islamic context, and not just in rural communities. I was attending meetings of small businessmen's associations in the markets where I was doing my dissertation research, and every meeting began with readings from the Qur'an. The *bismillah* ("in the name of God") initiated everything. If you were not ready for that oath, or not accustomed to it, you were excluded. I remember attending an academic conference at the University of the Gezira in Wad Medani, where I came to teach three years after Ustadh Mahmoud's execution. I had been invited to present a paper at a small seminar, and the proceedings were ostensibly in

English. Everyone participating in the meeting was a man, and everyone referred to or addressed each other as *al-akh,* "brother," except for me: I was not known to the group and was referred to as "Mr. Steve." But I did have one colleague in attendance, and his consciousness was raised by the clear manner in which I had been excluded by the language of the others. He began to refer to me in his remarks about my paper as *al-akh Steve,* to raised eyebrows around the table.

Islam is also vivid in language. I recall having an intense political conversation in Sudanese Arabic with an acquaintance who was a well-known stalwart of the Sudan Communist Party, Africa's oldest communist party. We absolutely could not converse in his mother tongue without using the name of God in virtually every sentence. Exclamations and verifications could not be made in Arabic without acknowledging the Almighty. "Wow!," "Really?" and "My goodness!"—all become intimately associated with God even in a historical-materialist context.

The era of political Islam or politicized Islam meant that even an organization that eschewed politics would be sucked into the fray. And Mahmoud Mohamed Taha and his followers could not stand by idly and simply observe the implementation of Islamic law in Sudan, a threat that Mahmoud had been warning of for thirty years. The core values of the Republican Brotherhood were based on the Qur'anic verse, *la ikrah f'il din,* "no compulsion in religion." After Ustadh Mahmoud's retreat in Rufa'a in the early 1950s, from which he emerged with the outline for *The Second Message of Islam,* he had stated that he would not isolate himself from Sudan society again, and he had taught his followers the essence of living an exemplary Muslim life in the midst of a modernizing society with all of its disturbances and upheavals. Ustadh Mahmoud's critique of Sudan's Sufi sects was largely about their artificial removal of themselves from a churning society; they were hiding behind their traditions. The struggle was to be of and in the world while entirely focusing on God at the same time, and balance was the achievement. There is a saying of the Prophet Mohamed that goes something like, "Even if the Day of Judgment has been called and you are in the midst of planting a palm tree seedling, finish that planting." The implication being that palm trees take many years to grow. Ustadh Mahmoud understood how to conduct his life in this way, and his followers were earnest apprentices. The political events that led to the end of that life exemplified Ustadh Mahmoud's unwavering consistency and tested his followers' faith in every way.

Sudan's President Jaafar Nimeiry imposed his version of Islamic law in September 1983, hence the sobriquet, "September Laws." Islamic law is set by Islamic jurists who interpret the Qur'an and the life of the Prophet Mohamed for applications to all aspects of daily life. Nimeiry's version featured the *hadd* punishments of amputations for thievery, and so on. Nimeiry staged a "photo op" for the occasion by pouring thousands of bottles of "sherry," a fortified wine manufactured in a factory in Khartoum North, into the Blue Nile, not far from his office in the Republican Palace. Alcohol would no longer be served in Sudan's Islamic republic.

It is thought that it was Ustadh Mahmoud who came up with the name "September Laws" for Nimeiry's version of sharia, in order to dissociate these policies from authentic "Islamic law." Since his participation in Sudan's struggle for independence, Mahmoud Mohamed Taha had stood for common sense in the intersection between the laws imposed by God and humankind. He stood for human freedom, and his first instance of resistance was when the British imposed laws against female circumcision in Sudan, where it was (and still is) widely practiced. The colonial officials described Ustadh Mahmoud as a "crazy fekki" for his leading a demonstration that would free the woman the British had charged with the crime of circumcising her daughter. Mahmoud's point, again, was not to trumpet the practice of female circumcision, but rather to speak out against the British attempting to legislate Sudanese morality as they continued to try to answer "the native question." This was a deep point, a subtle point, and related to Ustadh Mahmoud's concern that Sudan's women be offered the education that would put them in a position to make up their own minds to end this dangerous traditional practice. With education and transformative knowledge of faith, in Mahmoud's view, an individual could be the best judge of what God expected of him or her on Earth.

It was the same case with the Sudan government's imposition of the September Laws. Ustadh Mahmoud felt that Sudan was not in a position to implement such laws, particularly when a third of the population was not Muslim and would be haphazardly subjected to these laws, and the discrimination that Southern Sudanese already felt for not being Muslim in Sudan would be intensified. Taha also felt strongly that the Sudan government did not have the competence in Islamic affairs to administer even Nimeiry's version of laws construed to reflect Islamic principles. Another issue was the intent behind the imposition of Islamic law, which the Republicans viewed as more of a blatant political move by Nimeiry and his supporters in the Muslim Brotherhood to distract the nation from its increasing economic distress and raise its status in the Muslim world than a genuine expression of reverence or piety.

Mahmoud Mohamed Taha's concern for the unity of Sudan was a priority as well. The quest for some kind of autonomy in southern Sudan and the bloody war in the South had destroyed unity in Sudan since the early 1950s. Peace would not prevail with laws that the southerners would not tolerate, Sudan's global dignity and image were at stake, and millions of lives were at risk in the continuing war.

The imams of Khartoum's mosques, who were mostly employees of the national Ministry of Religion, began to speak out against the Republican position on the Islamist direction of the country. On the face of it, the imams' argument was an easy one to support. Standing up against an ostensibly "Islamic" government policy was subtle and required study to comprehend; it certainly could not be communicated in a sound bite. The brothers and sisters worked hard to represent themselves as decent, peace-loving Muslims, dedicated to lives of devotion. The sisters were particularly careful, acting discreetly and always seen in public in groups wearing their white taubs. But the perception of being "against Islam" was difficult to fight, and the Khartoum rumor mill broadcast whatever calumny could be imagined about Ustadh Mahmoud and his followers. Ustadh Mahmoud and the Republicans talked about morals, corruption, honesty, love, and cooperation, but much of the wider society only heard the innuendo about the movement. The rumor that Mahmoud "didn't pray" carried a great deal of currency in the context of his allegedly being "against sharia." This list of his "sins" combined with gossip about what all those women were doing in his house worked together to create a dangerous impression of the Republicans at that time. Non-Republican Sudanese of my acquaintance told me that they were concerned about my soul because I hung out with the Republicans. Or they shook their heads in amusement at my situation.

Without access to any form of mass media the Republicans organized themselves into a phalanx of public speakers to address small crowds in the streets about their concerns about the government's increasing Islamist orientation. As the shrill denouncement of the Republicans from the pulpits of urban mosques continued, the Republican speaker list was expanded to include as many as were capable of addressing the Republican position against "Islamic fanaticism" in Sudan. Every day and one by one, the brothers and sisters went to corners around town to denounce the government's Islamization of the country, and one by one they were arrested by the *jehaz al-amn al gowmi,* the national security police, until about seventy of the brothers and sisters were in prison.

This small, peaceful brotherhood, with virtually no infra-structure to speak of, was methodically and quickly taken apart by the government's national security police. The pursuit of the Republicans was harsh and cruel, and designed to scare off any other dissident movement in the country rather than actually enter into dialogue with what the Republicans were trying to say. What fascinated me was the elation that this crackdown evoked from the brothers and sisters not yet in prison. Many Republicans were convinced at this time that these arrests, this seeming national focus on Ustadh Mahmoud and his theology, would be the signal for the Messiah to return to Earth to im-plement God's judgment. With news of each arrest of a brother or sister who had been speaking out that day, the reaction from some was, "The time is coming!!" I was awed by this response, and frankly, nonplussed. I did not know what would happen next, or what would happen to me.

This is where my reluctance to say that this memoir is about me becomes acute. My dear friends were being arrested, the com-munity I had come to love was being destroyed, and I suddenly felt ambivalent about whether I was a part of this struggle or not. I felt inadequate, of course, and probably that I did not have the political, emotional, sociological, or spiritual resources to make sense of this situation and manage it for myself and those around me. I loved the Islam that I had learned from the Republicans, but I also felt that this was becoming a national political struggle in which I did not have a legitimate role, and whose arguments I certainly could not articulate very well. I watched and listened as carefully as I could, but I was anxious about the future of the Republican community.

The security police proceeded to work with the landlords of the four brothers' houses and have us evicted in July–August 1983. We wanted to stay in Thawra, near the center, the home of Ustadh Mahmoud, so we (the brothers' houses' occupants who had not been arrested) moved in with beds, boxes, and suitcases to the two health clinics that had been established not long before these events and run by brothers who were physicians. We slept and ate cheek-by-jowl in the clinic's courtyard, and brothers continued to go to work from one of the clinics or to report for duty in the public-speaking arena on a daily basis. It was clear to me that the brothers who went to the front line to speak out against the government's Islamist orientation were positive that they would be arrested, looked forward to joining their comrades in prison, and gladly accepted this mission.

In order to get a little more space and take care of the homes of brothers who were now in prison, some of us moved out of the clinic and into one or another of those houses. I was with maybe three or four brothers in such a house in Thawra, trying to focus on my research, when there was a knock on the door. It was a group of security police checking on the houses of the arrested brothers, and the look on their faces when they found me there was stunning. I remember the incident well when they recovered their composure after discovering a foreigner in the den of the "heretics," and with a certain swagger one of the policemen asked me, "If you are Muslim say *la ilaha li allah*" (the central Muslim creed of "there is no God but God."). I was proud of myself for finding a bit of my own swagger—with the security police no less, and I replied, "Yes I can say that, but not because you want me to." I apparently was asking for trouble, and with that they pushed me and one of the brothers who was also staying in the house with me into the back of a pickup truck and drove us from Thawra through Omdurman to Khartoum and their headquarters.

As we drove through neighborhoods where I had lived and had been conducting my interviews with tailors and other small-scale entrepreneurs, I remember thinking to myself clearly, particularly as we drove over the Nile Bridge connecting Omdurman with Khartoum, "I will probably be on a plane tonight, deported from Sudan." Given all that had happened to the brothers and sisters who were now in prison, the eviction from our houses, and the determination of the government to silence the Republicans, at that moment, on the back of the truck, a certain calmness came over me. I could not imagine an alternative scenario to my being deported, and I feel guilty now in reporting it, but I did think seriously about my own fate: "How am I going to finish this damn dissertation??" I must have had an appreciation for the basic decency of the Sudanese at that point, despite the fact that the two of us were being guarded in the back of the truck by security officers holding rifles. People in the neighborhoods where I had worked certainly stared at us as we drove by, but I figured I would not see them again, so, so what if they knew that I was being arrested?

My sense of that Sudanese decency was tested when we reached the security police headquarters and ushered into the "religious organizations section," where a senior woman officer interrogated both of us together in her small office. She proceeded to humiliate my friend who had a lighter complexion, with "Are you Sudanese?" repeated to him over and over again. She even asked *me* if he was Sudanese, and I decided to pretend I could not understand Arabic: my quickly devised clever plan to avoid incriminating anyone. With that, she launched into broken English, asking me about and then accusing me of funneling CIA money into the Republican Brotherhood.

This was a startling new tactic, and all I could think about and make jokes about later was that if I was a CIA agent living like this with the Republican brothers, the CIA was a very low-budget operation. If it were true, I would have been the most *miskeen* (pathetic) and dusty of CIA undercover operatives. When I stared blankly at her CIA accusations, the security officer then started to dive into her main agenda: using me to find key senior leaders of the Brotherhood. She wanted addresses and current locations, in "hiding" she assumed. I feigned ignorance, and three hours later the security people let me go by bus back to Omdurman.

I reported to the home of Ustadh Mahmoud, and he listened attentively to my brief story of detention. The brother who was arrested with me, Hamid a-Nil, was taken to the prison with the brothers who had been detained for their public speaking out against Islamization in Sudan. I have no recollection of where I slept that night, but I do remember a couple of weeks later, again staying in the home of one of the brothers who had been arrested early on in this crackdown, when I again answered a knock at the door and managed to again startle security police who were looking for other "fugitive" Republican Brothers.

This time they had me get into the back of a taxi, apparently the undercover vehicle of choice of the security police. We made the short drive to Ustadh Mahmoud's house where they picked up Ahmed Dali, the public-speaker-in-chief of the Republicans, who had long been a target of the government's allies in the Muslim Brotherhood. They had been after him since his University of Khartoum student days because he was an important public face and voice of the Republicans. All the way to the security police headquarters, through Omdurman and over the Nile, Dali pleaded with the police to release me because I was "just an academic." I was not sure whether or not I was guilty of that status yet, but I did go over in my mind again what would happen if this was to be my last night in Sudan. Our joint interrogation was briefer this time and by more senior officials. Dali was quickly whisked off to join the other brothers in detention at Kober Prison, and I was told to go out in the courtyard and sit on the manicured green lawn there, a new experience for me in the dry savannah land that was Khartoum.

The security police confiscated my passport and after about three hours, in which I fell asleep on the cool grass, an officer came out to talk to me, gave me a glass of water, and sat next to me on the ground, Sudanese style. He was different from those in my previous encounters in these offices. He seemed genuinely concerned that I was young and had converted to a "false path" in Islam, and he wanted to get me back on the right track. He told me that what I had been learning from the Republicans was not Islam and that there was "no originality" in Islam, and that I had fallen under the influence of "radical Sufis." An important component of the Republicans' understanding of Ustadh Mahmoud's teachings was that he had a unique perspective on God derived from his own intense spiritual quest. "Special knowledge" was extremely controversial in Islam and was sourced in the Sufi mystics who had made such claims in earlier centuries. Ustadh Mahmoud did not make these claims, but it was assumed he had this knowledge from his behavior, from what he said, and from his careful adherence to the path of the Prophet.

Ustadh Mahmoud's modern thinking was what had attracted me in good part to the Republican Brotherhood, but it was an enormously controversial part of his teaching as well. The progressive idea at the core of his thinking was that there was little point to being Muslim if you did not improve or deepen your understanding of the faith with each passing day. The naked fact was that Ustadh Mahmoud and the Republican brothers and sisters were *trying* with each new day to be better Muslims, to get closer to God. The Republican perspective on their fellow Muslims around the world was that non-Republicans sincerely believed that all they needed to do was to believe in the One God and His Prophet and pray their five prayers faithfully, and heaven would be guaranteed. This conflict over "special knowledge" was an excellent excuse for Sudan President Nimeiry to get rid of Ustadh Mahmoud.

Mahmoud Mohamed Taha's independence project was a spiritual one. Since the days of his Republican Party at the end of colonial Sudan, he had focused on independence as self-transformation, making a blatant effort to disrupt the continuance of tradition advocated by the bigger rival parties, the Ummah Party of the Mahdists and the Democratic Unionist Party tied to the Khatmiya Sufi sect. Both of these parties in fact were founded by traditional Sudan Sufi organizations. Transforming Sudan into an independent republic, all of whose citizens would learn to be democratic and form a democratic society, was Mahmoud's goal. Mahmoud's originality was in evidence from the beginning of his public career. "Freedom for us and for everyone," was the motto he gave to his Republican Party. It was a freedom that one worked on oneself, transforming oneself through prayer. But one needed an *atmosphere* of freedom to do that, not one compelled through sharia. The imposition of sharia in Sudan would be very much the *dhikir bidun fikr* (remembering God without really thinking about Him) line that the Republicans had always used against traditional Sufism.

On this my second visit to security police headquarters, which ironically was located across the railroad tracks from the American Club where I would occasionally scarf down my own comfort food—a hamburger with fries—the police released me in the middle of the night and left me on my own to find transport back to Thawra. I reached the blue door of Ustadh Mahmoud's house late and knocked softly. The brother who opened the door ushered me in, and we sat with a small group who listened to my latest tale of interrogation. I also learned that Ustadh Mahmoud himself had been arrested a few hours after Dali and myself, June 9, 1983, and had been taken off to detention. I left the house sadly and wondered where I could stay next; I still had my research to do.

One of the brothers who had been at the home of Ustadh Mahmoud when I got back from the security police told me to come and stay at his house, not far from that of Ustadh Mahmoud. I accepted his natural and generous offer gladly, while also remembering he had a wife and three small children with a fourth on the way. He had been an officer in Sudan's military and a Muslim Brother, so his own life as a Republican was one of remarkable transformation. I remember so many conversations with him over the two to three months I stayed in his house. He and other brothers were concerned that I was wavering from the Republicans, given that I was foreign and had been subjected to various recent indignities by Sudan's government. One close friend came by the house to sit with me to make sure I was okay physically as well as spiritually. As he left, he looked at me straight in the eye and told me in no uncertain terms, "There is absolutely nothing wrong with the Republican ideology." I was not sure that he wasn't trying to convince both of us.

Many of these conversations were in the evening in the dark, sitting in the courtyard trying to catch a cool breeze since the electricity was out for weeks at a stretch in Khartoum. Problems were caused by the summer rains silting the electricity-generating Blue Nile dam at Sennar. The man who had taken me in taught me the amazing trick of making cool water to drink by pouring it into the shallow aluminum tray that was used to carry food from the kitchen to where it was to be eaten. We worked on my transformation while watching the cooling power of evaporation.

The brothers checking on me did not seem to realize that in fact if anything my solidarity with them had been strengthened through my bit part in their life-altering drama. I had come to Sudan seeking total immersion in a Sufi community, and I found it. I could not be sure that the government wouldn't look for me again, but I also very much understood that I, unlike my brothers and sisters, could leave Sudan any time I wanted to, or as soon as I applied for a new passport. I personally felt safe there—it was my friends that I was very worried about. The Sudan government showed me that its right hand did not know what its left hand was doing. After receiving a new passport at the US Embassy, where I had explained that I had lost the old one, I had no problem getting a year's extension on my research visa from the government of Sudan.

In addition to applying for a new passport and assuring everyone that I was solidly with them, I also tried to keep busy during this time by continuing to collect data and conduct interviews with the tailors, metalworkers, and carpenters who were the subjects of my dissertation. Apparently no one recognized me from my appearance at gunpoint in the back of a security police pickup truck. My research assistant Shams and I went out to the markets every day to do this work, but it was hard because we were anxious about what might happen next and sad to have so many of the brothers and sisters in prison. The reports we received from the prisoners were very positive, however. We heard that they were all kept together, sharing a Republican compound as it were, in the political section of Kober (named after British colonial official "Cooper") Prison in Khartoum North. Sudan had a long history of jailing political prisoners, but also of releasing them, many of whom would then move back into positions of power in the country.

The brothers in Kober reported that they could cook their own food and have meetings featuring inshad, and they reported that their prison guards would stop by to listen to the singing. Virtually all Sudanese are from Sufi backgrounds, so the guards would appreciate the Republican medeh, the common term for inshad. Some of the best Republican inshad singers were in the prison group, in addition to most of the leadership of the organization. The prisoners reported elation in their cause and that the movement was now moving quickly to fulfill its dream of the end of the Nimeiry regime and his sharia, and the coming of a thousand years of peace on Earth. We frequently heard that the brothers in prison said that they were far happier than those of us on the outside. Their families, however, were starting to suffer from the absence of breadwinners among them. The four sisters in prison reported satisfaction with the work they were doing there, despite the fact that the women were not in a comfortable political section. They were in detention in the Omdurman Women's Prison with the prostitutes and illegal beer-brewers.

Ustadh Mahmoud was treated reasonably well in detention, kept separate from the other brothers in a small house near the security police compound. He was allowed to have food brought to him daily from his own home by one of the brothers, and he was taken for medical and dental appointments to the military hospital in Omdurman. The remarkable Sudan-style informality of the security process meant that brothers and sisters on the outside occasionally had opportunities to see Ustadh Mahmoud as he was driven to one or another of these appointments, because someone on the inside had given them the heads-up about his schedule. I believe notes between him and some of his followers were exchanged as well during this time.

I decided to seek the relative peace away from the capital and take a break in Rufa'a. But there I found anxiety and sadness as well among the Republican families whose sons and daughters were in jail. My peace was broken there too when the security police arrived to arrest my dear friend, Mowtasim. He was a prominent citizen of Rufa'a, farmer and former teacher, and lifelong Republican whom we called *omda* (mayor) because of his leadership in the community. He was taken to the prison in Wad Medani, the district headquarters, and was the sole Republican held there. Mowtasim was the only brother I had a chance to visit in prison. The informality outside of Khartoum apparently extended to allowing foreigners to visit political prisoners. I think we just sat together mostly in sad silence during my visit. I remember the high whitewashed walls of the courtyard where we sat. The only part of the outside world visible to us was the blue sky.

As the months of detention wore on, the Republicans began to make efforts to bring this situation to the attention of the world. The arrests were not reported in the government-controlled media in Sudan, but short pieces appeared elsewhere in Arab media. An appeal was made to Amnesty International to adopt Mahmoud Mohamed Taha and the imprisoned Republicans as Prisoners of Conscience. And a senior leader in Kober Prison, Ustadh Abdel Latif Omer, who had had a long career at one of Khartoum's newspapers, was recognized by the Committee to Protect Journalists in New York.

Using my status as a Fulbright Scholar (although my dissertation research grant had ended by this time), I managed to get a brief stand-up-in-the-hallway meeting with US Ambassador Hume Horan. He was aware of the repression and arrests of the Republican Brotherhood by the Sudan government, he told me, and he had had a meeting with a few other representatives of Western countries in Khartoum about the case. But the US government was also more interested in Sudan's stability because of an enormous refugee population, the world's largest at the time. There were refugees and displaced persons from severe drought in the region, and in the west of Sudan from rebellions in Chad. There was a huge group of refugees in Sudan's eastern regions from the long conflict over Eritrea's struggle for independence from Ethiopia.

Suddenly and unexpectedly, after eighteen months in detention, Ustadh Mahmoud and all of the brothers and sisters were released in mid-December 1984, days after I had left Sudan. Little time was spent celebrating, however. Within days of their release, the Republicans had written and published a one-page statement, "Either This or the Flood" (see appendix), which they then distributed by hand all over the Khartoum area.

The pamphlet was politely worded, referring to itself as "genuine and honest advice." It was a plea that essentially echoed the talks on the street that had resulted in the imprisonment of the brothers and sisters, calling for an end to Nimeiry's September Laws. And it summarized Republican critique of these laws—which included ancient punishments like severing the hand of a thief—as (1) an insult to all of Sudan's people, further damaging the relationship with the South, and (2) a technically flawed document in terms of its Islamic understanding, which would make it inoperable.

The government's reaction was swift. It arrested Ustadh Mahmoud again along with four of the brothers who had been distributing the document. They were now charged under Islamic law with the capital crime of apostasy (*rida*). It was hard to imagine five people less guilty of this crime. Apostasy was a Muslim's repudiation of his or her faith. Once a Muslim, always a Muslim. The previous period of detention had not involved any charges, but the Sudan government had now organized itself to make a proper example of Ustadh Mahmoud and his followers, manipulated the definition of the crime to fit its purpose, including the "violation" of the now-imposed September Laws, and quickly brought the alleged apostates to trial.

The trial took place at the beginning of January 1985, shortly after Sudan's independence day holiday. The brothers and sisters organized themselves to march to the courthouse in Omdurman the day of the trial in national dress, white jellabiyas and turbans for the brothers and the sisters in their white taubs. This was a video-recorded show trial. Ustadh Mahmoud represented himself with calm dignity, stating essentially that his accusers had no Islamic grounds to charge him with this crime. The only witness for the government's prosecution was a police officer who had arrested one of the brothers for distributing the flyer. Taha and his four disciples/co-defendants were convicted after a less than two-hour trial, with the verdict pronounced the next day. Under the arcane rules of apostasy convictions in sharia law, the convicted is generally given an opportunity to recant his "beliefs." Mahmoud Mohamed Taha would not recant, stating that all he had written and said was true. President Nimeiry declared him to be an "unrepentant apostate." He was taken to Kober Prison to await his sentence.

On Friday, the traditional day for Islamic executions, just two days after his conviction, Ustadh Mahmoud was led to the gallows in the courtyard of Kober Prison, which was filled with thousands of people. He refused a final statement, and as the canvas bag was slipped over his head, he had a smile on his face. On January 18, 1985 in the name of sharia, sharia law was violated by the execution of an elderly man, Mahmoud Mohamed Taha, aged seventy-six. His body was placed in a canvas body bag and hauled onto a helicopter that had landed in the prison courtyard. The helicopter flew off, and a crew of Kober prisoners buried his body in the desert, so that no funeral could be held, no construction of a memorial shrine. The story was reported on the front page of the *New York Times* the next day. Many of the Republican brothers and sisters, entire families, were rounded up by the police as the execution was taking place and held behind bars in extremely crowded cells in local police precinct offices. They were devastated by the loss of their most beloved teacher, and now they were jailed for several days. The four brothers who had been convicted with Ustadh Mahmoud were forced to recant his teachings on national television the Sunday after the execution. The tape was a difficult one to watch.

Seventy-six days later, April 6, President Jaafar Nimeiry was overthrown in a popular uprising that had filled Khartoum's streets with every description of worker and citizen. Sudan's 1985 intifada was led by a coalition of the forces that wanted to see peace in the South, as well as an end to Nimeiry's repression, and which had also opposed Taha's execution. Nimeiry at the time was visiting President Ronald Reagan in the White House, who was thanking Nimeiry for his assistance in securing the safe passage through Sudan earlier in the year for the Felasha Jews from Ethiopia to Israel.

During Sudan's intifada government, which followed, lasting until 1988, Asma Mahmoud, the daughter of Ustadh Mahmoud and a lawyer by training, brought a case to Sudan's Supreme Court. She won her case, overturning the apostasy conviction of her father, returning the property to the family, and restoring the marriage of her mother to her father. As Ustadh Mahmoud was a convicted apostate, his wife had been automatically divorced from him, as a Muslim woman cannot be married to a non-Muslim man. The post-Nimeiry Supreme Court had of course confirmed that Mahmoud's conviction as an apostate was not lawful.

Memory is an incomplete and complex phenomenon in Sudan. Trying to complete memory is the dominant mode of discourse among Republicans following the execution of their teacher. One will say, "Do you remember when Ustadh Mahmoud said . . . ?" and the other fills in the blanks, elaborates, revises. During a visit with Republican brothers and sisters in Ustadh Mahmoud's home town of Rufa'a in 2006 I attended a meeting where a letter was read containing remarkable detail of his execution, detail I had not heard in the twenty years previously. The letter was from a Kober Prison guard, relating his impressions of that day. He described how Ustadh Mahmoud's lifeless hand had fallen out of the body bag into which he had been placed after being removed from the scaffold. The guard had placed it gently back in the bag before it was lifted onto the helicopter. The small audience listened to the letter in stunned silence of grief or wept softly as the guard's recounting completed what had been the most horrific memory of all of the listeners' lives. The thought which was not given voice was of the astonishing news of the last person to have physically touched their teacher before he was taken from them. Their "grammar of pain"[1] did not include the words to describe that sense right then. But their futures were filled with conversations that sought the right word, making them and the man ever more complete.

Epilogue

Freedom

God is with the patient ones.

When Ustadh Mahmoud received visitors at his home he would often send them off with a hand-ful of dates, always in an odd number. Not four or six; it was usually seven. Odd numbers have more power than even numbers; there is a saying of the Prophet that makes this point. Aspects of ablution are in threes—washing the hands or face three times, for example. And the night prayer, *raka'a,* a set of bowing and pros-trating, is done in odd numbers. Odd numbers are off-center, less expected, raise questions. When we find an odd number of something, we humans might add one to restore balance. Odd numbers are incomplete, unfinished, suggestive of possibility. Ustadh Mahmoud's every action was full of meaning.

As this book developed into chapters at six-even, I saw the need for a seventh, an epilogue, in keeping with my theme here of listening to an unexpected voice out of Africa. An epilogue also allows me to scan the lives of the Republican brothers and sisters in the aftermath of the teacher's execution. I mentioned in an earlier chapter my own devotion to traveling to see my brothers and sisters in Sudan and almost wherever else they have landed: Egypt, the Arab Gulf, locations in Europe, and across the United States, of course. In many cases, under the circumstances of global economic and political change, I have managed to see some Republican families in multiple countries as they struggled to settle where they could find work and peace. I could certainly do another book on the Republicans' collective efforts to maintain their footing on the Path of the Prophet, to remember and savor every moment of the days of the movement, and to pass what they knew of Ustadh Mahmoud on to their children. This is a community of men and women whose lived experience of the rise of intolerance from within the Muslim ummah has intensified their awareness of the next spot on the globe that could erupt with the violence of ignorance, opportunism, or expediency.

But in 1988, three years after the execution of Mahmoud Mohamed Taha, I could not stay away from Sudan, so I took a leave of absence from my new job at Ohio University and accepted a Fulbright visiting lecturer position in the Department of Rural Development, University of the Gezira in Wad Medani. I chose this location because of my own interest in African socioeconomic development, the focus of this new university, and because I could be close to the brothers and sisters in Medani. And Medani is a bit upstream on the Blue Nile from Rufa'a, the small town I considered to be my spiritual home. The Republican community in Medani was led by Ustadh Saeed Sha'ib, a large man with a generous laugh who had a warm hug for everyone. With Ustadh Mahmoud as the Republican Brotherhood guide and teacher, Ustadh Said was considered to be the head of the organization, although he had not been designated as Ustadh Mahmoud's successor or spiritual heir.

I regularly walked from my house on the campus of the University of the Gezira to visit with Ustadh Saeed and the brothers and sisters who gathered at his home in the oldest neighborhood of Medani, particularly to see visitors from other regions of the country who would stop and pay their respects to this hospitable man. Medani was on the routes to Khartoum from points east, west, and south in Sudan. I was not surprised one day when he asked if I would go into the center of town with him to meet someone. We went into his office, where he had worked as an accountant for years, and there he introduced me to Hajja Hafza, a woman of about fifty, who looked like she had been through some very difficult times.

Ustadh Said left me alone with her in his office, and I extended my hand in greeting, which she received by covering her hand with her worn-looking taub. This was meant as a gesture of respect from a woman, although I had usually interpreted it as a conservative practice indicating she did not want to break her own "purity" by touching a man. The Republican sisters did not do this; they always shook men's hands forthrightly, so I was not used to her old-fashioned custom.

As she started to talk, eyes downcast, and adopting a pleading tone that sobered me, I realized with a shock who she was. The last time I had seen Hajja Hafza she had not been wearing a taub but the khaki green uniform of an officer of the national security agency. She was the policewoman who had interrogated me on my first arrest for "being in the same house as Republicans" during the crackdown five years earlier in 1983. Hajja Hafza had kept insulting the brother who had been arrested with me, asking him repeatedly if he was in fact Sudanese. "Hajja Hafza" was, in effect, her nom de guerre, and it seems that all the political prisoners knew her by that name.

After the fall of the Nimiery regime in 1985, Hajja Hafza had fallen on hard times; she was relieved of her position in the security police agency, and she lost her husband. She asked me in a resigned tone if I could arrange for her a contact with the US embassy to see if she could get a visa to travel to the United

States, exiling herself and looking for better opportunities. I explained to her, and later to Ustadh Said, that I was not an employee of the embassy or the US government and had no *wasta* (influence) there.

When the two of us left the office and found Ustadh Saeed out in front waiting, she looked very tired and like she had absorbed so much disappointment there really wasn't room for more. Ustadh Saeed looked down at me—he was also very tall—with an expression as if he had been testing me, gently. He did not push the issue. And when I told him that I had recognized her, he simply explained her difficult circumstances and that he had wanted to see if there was anything I could do for her. And that was the end of the discussion about Hajja Hafza between the two of us.

However, when some of the brothers heard about this interview they were almost as surprised as I was. We must have been the cadre of the brotherhood not very evolved in our understanding of the need to let go and act in a conciliatory manner at all times. I was overwhelmed by the extension of Ustadh Saeed's generous spirit to this woman who had been an official responsible for his arrest and detention as well as that of the other brothers and sisters in prison. *Al-muamalat,* "good acts," in Republican thinking were not limited by who should receive them, because their primary function was to strengthen the believer's strides on the Path of the Prophet.

I had had a similar revelation about the Republican ability to try to see things in the most positive light a few years earlier while finishing up my doctoral studies at Michigan State University. I had returned to East Lansing from Sudan feeling bereft of Sudan and Republican Brotherhood connections, but I quickly found that there were a number of (non-Republican) Sudanese studying at MSU at that time. I started to attend some of their communal weekend suppers—definitely of the azaba (bachelor) variety—which helped keep my Sudanese Arabic in shape. The food that they prepared for themselves must have triggered nostalgia in these guys by its very shape, because the flavor certainly did not remind me of their mothers' cooking. One evening as we ate, one of these Sudanese graduate students mentioned that he thought so-and-so was "luuty." In my usual vocabulary-development mode I asked what that word meant. Everyone stopped and looked at me in surprise. "It means homosexual," one of the guys offered. Their surprise was in the fact that Sudan's vice president under Nimiery had been rumored to be homosexual; whether true or not, such an accusation was a distinct insult in that culture. All of these Michigan State Sudanese knew of my connection to the Republican Brotherhood, and that the then vice president had been in charge of the persecution of the Republicans. I knew from the brothers that the vice president had been responsible for the assault on the Republicans. But that no Republican had ever shared the rumor of his sexuality in my presence, despite the great harm that the vice president was doing to the brotherhood, was another mark of their live-and-let-live orientation.

What fascinated me was not so much that no Republican had shared this rumor with me, but that they did this as a natural matter of course—that it did not require "plotting to keep secrets from Steve." They were simply carefully following the *adab,* good manners or behavior that had been modeled and taught by Ustadh Mahmoud. Gossiping was not consistent with good manners. And these good manners are also to what I credit the lack of much "salty vocabulary" in my Sudanese Arabic; the only swearing I know is a strong *wallahi!* (my God!). These examples were further evidence of the Republican approach to life: Everything was religion and religion was everything. Each was a vital extension of the other, and if life and religion did not move in concert, the struggle to be a good Muslim did not have much meaning. And although politics was far down the list of priorities of the Republican Brotherhood, this position on religion and life needing to stay in sync was also their foundation for democracy. Behaving in this socially conscious manner was "being democratic with oneself" in the Republican view, the necessary initial starting point for implementing democracy in the wider society. Hypocrisy has been a concern of the Muslim ummah since the revelation of the Qur'an. Honest democracy with oneself was the antidote to hypocrisy with strong roots in the Republican Brotherhood's project for life.

A third incident that confirmed my sense of the wider society's consciousness of what had occurred in its midst with Mahmoud Mohamed Taha and the Republican Brotherhood took place in Aswan, Egypt, while I was on a 1994 sabbatical from Ohio University. I had traveled to Egypt hoping to get to Sudan, which I had not visited since the 1989 coup. Aswan was in many respects the next best thing in that its proximity to Sudan meant that Sudanese Arabic was the lingua franca—not that Egyptians would admit they were speaking Sudanese Arabic. The Nile's bluffs and islands, the High Dam, and the nearby astonishing monuments to Pharaoh Ramses on Lake Nasser, which could only be visited when accompanied by an Egyptian army convoy because of recent attacks on tourists, were only part of the drama of my stop in Aswan. I had gone to see Yassir Shukery, an Aswan lawyer and longtime Republican Brother whom I had met on an early trip to Atbara in my first months with the brotherhood.

Yassir's visit to Sudan was about a dozen years before my trip to Aswan. He brought with him on his Sudan trip a colleague of his, a fellow lawyer, who had said that he wanted to learn more about Ustadh Mahmoud and his approach to modern Islam. Yassir's colleague actually received a lot of good-natured ribbing during his trip to Sudan because he clearly had been "out of shape" vis-à-vis his religious practice, something that had been very obvious to everyone in a deeply religiously observant society.

In the year that followed Yassir and his colleague's visit to Ustadh Mahmoud and the Sudan Republicans, there was of course the government crackdown on the movement, the arrests of many brothers and sisters, and the execution of al-Ustadh. In Egypt, where government surveillance of the activities of religious organizations was far more rigorous than in Sudan, brother Yassir was arrested and thrown into jail for his membership in this Sudanese group, despite his minimal proselytizing on behalf of the Republican movement. It turned out that the colleague he had brought with him to Sudan was an informant for the Egyptian religious police, and he had turned Yassir in.

Although I knew that Yassir had been in jail for his link to the Republicans, I had forgotten the details. He also took me around to meet the handful of other Republicans in Aswan, including a remarkable man who had also served time in prison for his Republican affiliation despite the fact that he had never traveled to Sudan or met Ustadh Mahmoud. I told him how much I admired his faith. Yassir then took me to his Lawyers' Syndicate in Aswan to meet his colleagues, which I felt was as much about showing me off as the "Arabic-speaking Muslim khawaja," as anything else. But then as we sat sipping tea and chatting, a disheveled man came into the room and slowly approached me at the large wooden table in the Syndicate's hall.

He nervously shook my hand, bent down, and then hugged me tightly. He was Yassir's colleague who had turned him in to the police during the Republican crackdown. He cried, asked my forgiveness over and over again, and demonstrated deep shame for what he had done.

I was overwhelmed, of course, particularly by the idea that I was to receive these apologies and condolences on behalf of all the Republicans, in that I was the only one "from Sudan" whom this man had met since his trip to Omdurman. His remorse seemed genuine, and apparently he had lost both his lawyer job and his connection to the Egyptian government as these events unfolded on both sides of the border. I was struck once again by the evidence of those outside the Republican circle regretting their behavior toward it in the past.

Although I have never made a point of seeking a spot on the lecture circuit with talks about my experience with the Republican Brotherhood, I have many times accepted invitations from a wide range of groups of Sudanese people living in the United States to talk about the era of Mahmoud Mohamed Taha. I always adamantly stress my lack of expertise as a theologian or even a historian, but I think that the Sudanese have felt isolated from the world by the behavior of their government over the past four decades or so; that reaching out to someone who might have something positive to say makes them feel better about themselves. It has also been clear to me that Sudanese in exile are fascinated about being able to converse with a blue-eyed khawaja in Sudanese Arabic, another example of African people feeling that there isn't much room in the world for their language when faced with the overwhelming hegemony of English. I remember in 2004 going to the Sudan Embassy in Washington to seek an entry visa and meeting the visa official who was sufficiently impressed with my command of his mother tongue to insist that I meet the ambassador. I was not very happy with this idea in that I had my own personal policy of avoiding Sudan government contact as much as possible after the persecution of the Republican Brotherhood and the execution of Ustadh Mahmoud. But I *was* in their embassy.

The ambassador asked me to sit down, offered tea, of course, and we had a pleasant conversation. He, in effect, interviewed me about my feelings about Sudan, and although I was as circumspect as possible, given the continuing atrocities in Darfur and the South, he did elicit from me a statement that I felt "safe" when I visited Khartoum. I was astonished a couple of weeks later to learn from friends in Khartoum that *"American professor feels safe in Khartoum"* appeared as a large newspaper headline, complete with my picture. So I became a propaganda tool in the midst of the Khartoum government's brutal crackdown on insurgents and noncombatant villagers in the western region of Darfur, described by world governments as genocide.

The brutality and the simple lack of opportunity in their home country have cast an enormous Sudanese diaspora out into the world, covering every corner of the Middle East and Europe, and my own specialty, the United States. Many in this community achieve great success abroad, doing better perhaps than they would have in Sudan. And many have led lives as survivors, driving taxis, working as security guards, or delivering pizza, trained with bachelor's degrees and beyond. My own interactions with them have covered the range of both of these groups, feeling a bit myself like part of the diaspora.

Republicans living in the United States have sought ways to remember their teacher, particularly around the anniversary of his execution, January 18. These events have become remarkable reunions for those living in the United States for years and orientation sessions for those either new to the movement or on brief trips to this country. We have held the memorial event twice in Athens, Ohio, where I live. The first time was when Ustadh Mahmoud was recognized by Ohio University's African Students Union as its African Hero in 2000, an annual event commemorating Nelson Mandela's release from prison in South Africa. And the second time was in 2009 when we organized a conference entitled "100 Years of Progressive Muslims" to mark what would have been Ustadh Mahmoud's 100th birthday.

A few years prior to the latter conference I had been browsing in a large bookstore, and came across the latest essay collection from Cornel West, *Democracy Matters: Winning the Fight against Imperialism* (2004). Glancing at the index, I was astonished to discover several references to "Taha, Mahmoud Mohamed." I bought the book and immediately asked Abdullahi Ahmed An-Na'im if he had introduced West to the thought of Ustadh Mahmoud, but he was as surprised as I to learn of what West had written. I of course knew of Cornel West's intellectual power and his extensive writings on racism in the United States, but I could not trace his interest in the work of Mahmoud Mohamed

Taha. At the beginning of a year's worth of preparation for our "progressive Muslims" conference, the Republican community in the United States in effect dared me to go after Cornel West for the conference keynote. I approached the challenge in a guileless manner, figuring that the worst he could say was (and that his probable response would be) "no, thanks."

But after a year of back-and-forth with West's agent and a last-minute drama involving President Obama's first inauguration (West was, in early 2009, a big fan of the president's and had been invited to a pre-inaugural breakfast; we had to change the time of West's keynote to accommodate his need to get to Washington for that event), Professor Cornel West indeed keynoted our conference on "progressive Muslims" and earned a loud ovation from a standing-room-only audience in Ohio University's Baker Center Ballroom.

We had made a short documentary about the life of Mahmoud Mohamed Taha for the conference and included in the film some of what West had written about Ustadh Mahmoud: "Taha conceives of Islam as a holistic way of life that promotes freedom—the overcoming of fear—in order to pursue a loving and wise life" (*Democracy Matters,* 140). The crowd gathered for the keynote went wild, and West asked me for two copies of the film, one for his mother. In his thundering talk Cornel West elevated Mahmoud Mohamed Taha to the Pantheon of Gandhi, Martin Luther King Jr., and Nelson Mandela, which was certainly not news to the Republican brothers and sisters gathered for the event. But this did provide better context for my many students and colleagues in attendance than I had ever managed to produce in one of my lectures. Cornel West understood what the Republicans admired most about Ustadh Mahmoud—his love of freedom—something he shared with Gandhi, King, and Mandela. I most recently heard Cornel West invoke the name of Mahmoud Mohamed Taha while a panelist in 2015 on the Bill Maher Show's confusing "attack and defense of Islam and

Muslims" discussion about the current "Islamic State" violence in Syria and Iraq. It reminded me of my awkward conversation with Ustadh Mahmoud that afternoon in 1982 when I asked him naively for more "freedom" from the obligations of attending all of the many meetings of the brotherhood. His response was to tell me that some day people all over the world would come to the Republican idea. I'm just beginning to understand what he meant.

I was asked to speak to a meeting of the Sudanese *ja'alia* (community living abroad) in Philadelphia in early 2013. I read them sort of a half-English, half-Sudanese Arabic translation of the first chapter of this book. They were doctors, pharmacists, taxi drivers, teachers, and store clerks gathered in the basement function room of an anonymous motel in North Philly, determined to keep in touch with each other in the big American city. They were not Republicans but they got my Sudan jokes, were moved by the tender details, and nodded knowingly at the Sufi stories. They reacted to the humaneness and realized that they had missed something or not paid attention in their past lives as workers or university students in Khartoum. They made the bitter contrast with the state of Sudan today, determining that extremism had driven their country to ruin. This group of forty to fifty middle-aged Sudanese men and women who had exiled themselves to chilly Philadelphia for economic and political reasons now saw some relevance in the work of Ustadh Mahmoud. Nostalgia was there, of course, as exile's companion. But they also expressed pride in Taha, seeing him now as a national hero.

Transcendent brotherhood was the life-giving agar that fueled the Republicans' positive outlook and brought them together. It was a focus on oneness as a goal of humanity, rather than on difference—either among Muslims or between Muslims and other faiths. It was a destination on the Path of the Prophet. Ustadh Mahmoud illustrated it beautifully in a remarkable interview he had in the early 1960s with John Voll. Voll is a well-known American historian of Sudan who had been conducting his dissertation research on the history of the Khatmiya, a Sufi order founded in the Kassala area. Sayed al-Hassan, the founder of this order, was a mystic revered by Republicans for his adherence to the Path of the Prophet. Voll had asked Ustadh Mahmoud about Islamic reform efforts, and he gave Voll a response redolent of the early space age: "The age-old dream of the human caravan is not to send astronauts in their orbit in the outer space. It is to send its individuals, every single individual, in his orbit of self-realization. It is high time that this dream be thus reinterpreted. It is also the sacred duty of every man and woman to help to intelligently reorientate [*sic*] human endeavor towards the culmination of this pilgrimage" (Republican Brotherhood pamphlet, "Questions and Answers," page 8).

Material like this, quotes from Ustadh Mahmoud—the sound bites of an earlier era—were an important part of the Republican identity. Brothers and sisters committed them to memory and published them in books and pamphlets to be sold on Sudan's streets as well as turned into posters to decorate their homes. But clearly the message did not reach very far into the wider Sudan society, drowned out by rumor, innuendo. and suspicion of unconventional "holy men." I am struck by what we have missed in overlooking small-scale, peaceful social movements and also struck by the circuitous ways in which such phenomena grab our attention once again.

The obstacle for the multitudes who may have overlooked what Ustadh Mahmoud and his followers were saying was the difficulty in penetrating the deep Republican message. It is also true that peace-loving, women-centric, and progressive movements don't attract much financial backing anywhere in the world. The response to John Voll above was perhaps meant as an invitation to possibility, expressed in English, rather than a summary of a complex theology. This is why the small-scale study group approach of the brotherhood—the intense learning exercises and opportunities they set up for themselves—yielded great solidarity, but you had to know the method.

I know that I have neglected my own obligations in spreading the good news of this movement. My excuse is clearly that I have never been completely confident that I understood it myself or understood enough to communicate its depth to others. I did understand that the Republicans wanted to spread their message not because they felt it superior, but rather, because their message promoted the oneness, a universal coming together across humankind. The irony is that thirty years earlier Omer El Garrai, known for his public speaking on behalf of the movement and later my Ohio PhD student, had given me a lot to think about when he jabbed me with a comment at a Republican farewell event for me. While the group was engaged in a Republican hymn, Omer leaned over to me and said in a low voice, "You just joined us in order to study us."

While at that moment I had found his comment painful in that I had felt that I had been participating sincerely and with more and more enthusiasm over the previous months, I have often wondered if I really would have understood Ustadh Mahmoud's work better if I *had* been studying it in an academic manner. What I do understand now is that my intention in membership with the Republican Brotherhood—a spiritual quest in solidarity with an African people—is the source of my inability today to gaze at Africans as the exotic "other." I work hard to get this stance across to my own students, particularly when teaching research methodologies. And this is my stance in my work to promote the study of Africa, its peoples, and languages from what is really an "Afro-centric" perspective, as means to learn about African ways to organize society that may be useful in the West. I always look at myself as a *learner*, not that I am the master of all knowledge of this enormous continent. My ability to understand Africa from this perspective I feel is—as much as anything—a tribute to the Republican brothers and sisters welcoming me into their community as nothing more than a fellow human being who wanted to join their quest.

The empty lot next to Ustadh Mahmoud's house in Omdurman, where the group held their evening meetings, was an apt metaphor for the Republicans' openness. They did not perceive any boundaries to the expansive ideology that they discussed in that empty lot and studied so carefully. Passersby were most welcome to stop and listen, or inquire.

As a teacher, the methodology proposed in Republican practice was attractive to me, an early lure to my joining the movement. The methodology has provided a significant context for me in which to think about what has happened to Sudan and this community since my life with them in the early 1980s, as well as a means to teach about Africa and the possibilities of social change. The methodology is the path to freedom, and it takes hard work. That hard work promotes remarkable solidarity.

On a 2006 visit to Sudan I spent a few days in Rufa'a with my friend and teacher, Khalid El Haj. He had invited a group of about eight people to his house for breakfast, commemorating the publication of his book, *Peace in Islam*. Most of the people sitting around Khalid's saloon had assisted in the publication process in some way. I remember the conversation that ensued as one of the most intensely intellectual experiences of my life because of the quality and equality of participation that fueled the discussion.

As a social scientist who has worked across Africa, I learned that what we can know best in a community is the agenda that people have for their own progress, and the questions that they have about how to make that progress. Ideally, this agenda presents itself naturally without probing or prodding; it emerges in conversation and listening. I was in the odd space of being dedicated to the Republican methodology and its practices while also trying to learn more about it—in effect, a researcher. It was my background, my history with these people that gave me the privilege of participating in Khalid's breakfast meeting and witnessing an emergent process.

Khalid El Haj was a leader of the movement who had also authored several of its important books. He joined the Republicans as a student in the 1960s. Because Rufa'a was Ustadh Mahmoud's hometown, Khalid had grown up with Republican thinking in his neighborhood and in close proximity to neighbors and family members who belonged to an array of Sufi sects. Khalid had been a patient teacher with me from the beginning of our friendship, helping me understand both big picture and nuance in Ustadh Mahmoud's perspective. The simple room in which this meeting was held contained three beds that functioned as sofas during the day, a wooden table, and a couple of wardrobes for books and clothing. There was a large photograph of Ustadh Mahmoud on the wall. Over the course of three hours, Khalid presented an informal lecture—guided by questions from his audience. His focus as he talked was on the intellectual process of a Republican brother, influenced, as he said, by Mahmoud Mohamed Taha, but not directed by him. But he also said, "Academic research is boring."

I wasn't wounded to the quick by that statement; I understood that he meant there was no room for anything called "objectivity" in this complicated world we were trying to understand. Everything had an unshakable point of view. You study the situation carefully and apprentice yourself to those whose vision you trust, who seemed to have the vision of human perfection in sight. I marveled at how this represented the seamlessness of oneness, that if the goal was to achieve this universal peace, then of course we all had to get on the same page. In the case of this breakfast session, all of us were already on that page, just looking for guidance in pronunciation or grammar, to extend the metaphor. The participants—host and guests—were all entirely engaged in the process of learning from one another.

The pilgrimage to oneness, what Ustadh Mahmoud called "this orbit of self-realization," could not be accomplished alone—at least initially. A supportive crowd was needed to keep you headed in the right direction and to serve as a buffer from the many dangers scattered along the path. The unifying experience is like prayer, which is also considered to be the best way to get ready for and to practice the focus needed to attain oneness. This is why Ustadh Khalid's small audience was energized and utterly focused that morning in Rufa'a. The concerns and aspirations of the audience were in complete alignment with those of the presenter; no outsider was mining a community for data. Khalid El Haj provided examples from the life and work of Ustadh Mahmoud and from his own encounter with that life. We all as participants could relate to the striving for *mezan,* a balance between this modern world and the tools of faith that equipped us for it, which Khalid's stories illustrated.

Since 1982 I have been a struggling student in an open classroom of lovers of freedom. My teachers have been my brothers and sisters, all of them always ready to push me to the next level. The unity of purpose among the Republicans has suffered blows throughout the movement's history, blows which may have dampened the spirits of some. But in no way does that diminish our need to pay attention to open and democratic initiatives in today's Muslim world. Go and look for them in peace.

Appendix

"Either This or the Flood"

This leaflet, printed in Arabic and English, was distributed in the Khartoum area in December 1984 and resulted in the arrests of five of the Republican Brothers, including Mahmoud Mohamed Taha.

In the name of Allah, the Beneficient, the Merciful

Either this or the Flood!

"And guard against a chastisement that will not befall the unfair
ones alone, and know that Allah is severe in punishment." (Surah 8, 25)

We, the Republicans, have dedicated our lives to the promotion and
protection of two honourable objectives, namely, Islam and the Sudan. To
this end we have propagated Islam at the scientific level which is capable
of resolving the problems of modern life. We have also sought to safeguard
the superior moral values and original ethics which Allah has conferred upon
this People, thereby making them the appropriate conveyer of Islam to the
whole of modern humanity which has no recourse nor dignity other than by
the means of this great Religion.

The September 1983 laws have distorted Islam in the eyes of intelligent members of our people and in the eyes of the world, and degraded the
reputation of our country. These laws violate Shari'a (Islamic law) and violate Religion itself. They permit, for example, the amputation of the hand
of one who steals public property, although according to Shari'a neither the
hud (specified) punishment nor any ta'zeer (discretionary) punishment may be
imposed in such cases because of the shubha (doubt) raised by the participation of the accused in the ownership of such property. These unfair laws
have added imprisonment and fine to the hud (specified) penalties in contra-
vention of the rationale and provisions of Shari'a. They have also humili-
ated and insulted the people (of this nation) who have seen nothing of these
laws except the sword and the whip, although they are a people worthy of all
do respect and reverence. Moreover, the enforcement of hudud and Qasas
(specified penalties) and retribution) presupposes a degree of individual education and social justice which is lacking today.

These laws have jeopardized the unity of the country and divided the
people in the north and south by provoking religious sensitivity which is
one of the fundamental factors that has aggravated the Southern Problem.
It is futile for anyone to claim that a Christian person is not adversely
affected by the implementation of Shari'a. A Muslim under Shari'a is the
guardian of a non-Muslim in accordance with the "verse of the sword" and
the "verse of jizia" (respectively, calling for Muslims to use arms to
spread Islam and impose a humiliating poll-tax on the subjugated non-Muslim
believers). They do not have equal rights. It is not enough for a citizen
today merely to enjoy freedom of worship. He is entitled to enjoy the full
rights of a citizen in total equality with all other citizens. The rights
of southern citizens in their country is not provided for in Shari'a, but
rather in Islam at the level of fundamental Qur'anic revelation i.e. the
level of Sunna. We therefore call for the following:

1. We call for the repeal of the September 1983 laws because
   they distort Islam, humiliate the People and jeopardize
   national unity.
2. We call for the haulting of bloodshed in the South and the
   implementation of a peaceful political solution instead of
   a military solution. This is the national duty of the government as well as the armed southerners. There must be the
   brave admission that the South has a genuine problem and the
   serious attempt to resolve it.
3. We call for the provision of full opportunities for the en-
   lightenment and education of this People so as to revive Islam
   at the level of Sunna (the fundamental Qur'an). Our times
   call for Sunna and not Shari'a. The Prophet, peace be upon
   him, said: "Islam started as a stranger, and it shall return
   as a stranger in the same way it started...Blessed are the s
   strangers! They said: Who are the strangers, Oh Messenger
   of Allah? He said: Those who revive my Sunna after it has
   been abandoned."

This level of Islamic revival shall achieve pride and dignity for
the People. In this level, too, lies the systematic solution for the
Southern Problem as well as the Northern Problem. Religious fanaticism
and backward religious ideology can achieve nothing for this People except
religious upheaval and civil war.

Here is our genuine and honest advice. We offer it on the occasion of the Christmas and Independence day anniversaries; and may Allah expedite its acceptance and safeguard the country against upheaval and preserve its independence, unity and security.

25th December 1984
2 Rabi Athany 1405 Hj

The Republican Brothers
Omdurman

Notes

Chapter 1: Unity

1. Mahmoud Mohamed Taha, *Religion and Social Development* (Omdurman: Republican Brotherhood, 1976).

2. Tim Niblock, *Class and Power in Sudan* (Albany: State University of New York Press, 1987), 126.

3. Abdullahi An-Na'im, "Resume of the Life of Mahmoud Mohamed Taha" (1983). This and other details of Mahmoud Mohamed Taha's early life are from a typescript prepared by An-Na'im while in prison. The document was meant for circulation to human rights groups during the detention of Republican brothers and sisters, including Mahmoud Mohamed Taha.

4. Khalid El Haj, "The Republican Party" (1996), typescript in Arabic, translation by Asma AbdelHalim.

5. Mahmoud Mohamed Taha, *Questions and Answers,* 2nd ed. (Omdurman, 1971), 10.

6. Khalid El Haj, "Republican Party."

7. Abdullahi Ahmed An-Na'im, Translator's Introduction to Mahmoud Mohamed Taha, *The Second Message of Islam* (Syracuse, NY: Syracuse University Press, 1987), 3.

8. SAD 525/11/12 8 October, 1946, by Hancock, #102, Sudan Archive, Durham University.

9. Mohamed Mahmoud, "Mahmud Mohamed Taha and the Rise and Demise of the Jumhouri Movement," *New Political Science* 23, no. 1 (2001): 72.

10. Mahmoud Mohamed Taha, *The Second Message of Islam,* trans. Abdullahi Ahmed An-Na'im (Syracuse, NY: Syracuse University Press, 1987), dedication page.

11. Awad al-Sid al-Karsani, "Beyond Sufism: the Case of Millennial Islam in the Sudan," in *Muslim Identity and Social Change in Sub-Saharan Africa,* ed. Louis Brenner (Bloomington: Indiana University Press, 1993), 135.

12. Richard Werbner, "Smoke from the Barrel of a Gun: Postwars of the Dead, Memory and Reinscription in Zimbabwe," in his *Memory and the Postcolony: African Anthropology and the Critique of Power* (London: Zed Books, 1998), 71–102.

13. Abdullahi An-Na'im, "Mahmoud Mohamed Taha and the Crisis in Islamic Constitutional Law Reform" (typescript, 1986), 30.

Chapter 2: The Path of the Prophet

1. Mahmoud Mohamed Taha, *The Second Message of Islam,* trans. Abdullahi Ahmed An-Na'im (Syracuse, NY: Syracuse University Press, 1987), 39.

2. Ibid., 61.

3. Daniel Martin Varisco, *Islam Obscured* (New York: Palgrave Macmillan, 2005), 152.

4. Taha, *Second Message of Islam,* 126.

5. Ibid., 138.

6. Ibid., 134.

7. Ibid., 137.

8. Ibid., 63.

Chapter 4: A Women's Movement

1. Interview with Mahmoud Mohamed Taha, 1970s, unpublished in Arabic.

2. Mahmoud Mohamed Taha, *The Second Message of Islam,* trans. Abdullahi Ahmed An-Na'im (Syracuse, NY: Syracuse University Press, 1987), 56.

3. Ibid., 140.

4. Taha, *Reform and Development of the Islamic Personal Law Shari'a,* trans. Einar Berg (Oslo, 1971), 82–83.

5. Ibid., 107.

6. Sudan's first female political prisoners were Sudan Communist Party members Fatima Ahmed and Niemat Malik among others, personal communication, Asma AbdelHalim, 2003.

7. Interview with Asma Mahmoud, Oxford, Ohio, 1996.

8. Letter from Mahmoud Mohamed Taha to Cultural Secretary, Khartoum University Student Union, September 17, 1979 (in Arabic).

9. Taha, *Reform and Development of the Islamic Personal Law,* 99.

10. Ibid., 99–100.

11. Taha, *Second Message of Islam,* 153.

12. Taha, *Reform and Development of the Islamic Personal Law,* 131.

13. Taha, *Second Message of Islam,* 140–41.

14. Ibid., 142.

Chapter 6: A Modern Muslim

1. Fiona Ross, *Bearing Witness: Women and the Truth and Reconciliation Commission* (London: Pluto, 2003), 3.

Glossary of Sudanese Arabic Terms

(N.B. The glossary reflects Sudan dialect of Arabic pronunciation: 'dh' is pronounced as 'z' in English; the a' represents the Arabic letter "ein," pronounced as a nasal *a*.)

abid	slave
adhan	call to prayer
adam	good manners
al-akh	brother
al-akhira	the Hereafter
al-duniya	this world
al-giwama	protection of women by men; a Qur'an concept
al-jama	the group
al-jelsa sabahiya	early morning meeting
Allah aa'lim	only God knows
al-mu'amalat	social transactions or good acts
al-mudhaf	divine document (a name for Qur'an)
al-mughrib	sunset prayer
al-muh'minun	the believers

al-towhid	monotheism
am	uncle
angareb	traditional bed of wood and woven sisal mat
arage	long shirt
aragi	home-brewed gin
arkan	pillars (of faith)
a-sadiq, al-muhubba, wa al-ikhlas	truth, love, and charity
asida	sorghum or millet porridge
asha	supper
asaya	sticks
asur	late afternoon
awra	the parts of a woman's body that should remain hidden from view
azaba	single men, bachelors
azraq	dark blue
ba'ati	a restless dead person
baraka	blessing
batin	hidden
berenda	veranda
beyt-al-akhwan	brothers' house
beyt-al-ukhwat	sisters' house
beyt azaba	bachelors' quarters
bida	innovation after the time of the Prophet
binaati mu'alafaati	"my daughters (women followers) are my writings"
bismillah	"in the name of God"

GLOSSARY OF SUDANESE ARABIC TERMS

buhur	incense
butana	plain
darwish	follower of a traditional Sufi master
dawa	mission for proselytizing
dhikir	remembrance/chanting the name of God
dhikir bidun fikr	remembering without much reflection
din	religion
fatwa	legalistic opinion
fatur	breakfast
fekki	religious mystic
fikr	ideology
fikr jumhuriya	the Republican Brothers' ideology
foul	long-simmered fava beans
gada	wooden bowl
ghafla	inattention/leisure
ghar	cave
gowm	community or group
giyam a-leyl	night prayer
hamla	campaign
haraka-t-al-mar'a	women's movement
hijira	migration
housh	courtyard
housh juwa	get inside the prayer
hudur	intense concentration in prayer
ibada	obligatory religious worship practice
ibreeks	containers for ablutions

GLOSSARY OF SUDANESE ARABIC TERMS

inshad	hymns
inshad erfani	spiritual poetry
ja'alia	community living abroad
jalous	mud construction material
jelsa	meeting, lit., "sitting"
jehaz al-amn al gowmi	national security police
jenaza	shrouded remains
Jihad	
jirjir	watercress
kaffir	unbeliever
karkedeh	drink made from dried hibiscus petals
khabir ajanabi	"foreign expert"
khalwa	place of retreat/meditation
khawaja	foreigner/Westerner
kisra	bread
la ikrah f'il din	"no compulsion in religion"
lateef	gentle, nice, kind, friendly, graceful
mafi din bidun angeen	"no religion without batter" (i.e., food)
mafi mushkila	"no problem"
marara	organ meat from a sheep
maulana	religious teacher
maseed	a Sufi school for Qur'an study
maseera	procession
mazoun	religious official presiding over marriage
medeh	traditional Sufi ode
merisa	sorghum beer, mildly alcoholic

GLOSSARY OF SUDANESE ARABIC TERMS

mezan	balance
mislaya	prayer rugs
miya-fi-miya	100 percent
mulah	okra-based sauce
munshid (pl. *munshidiin*)	one who has mastered singing of odes
mushtageen	"You've been missed."
mustajid	newcomer
omda	mayor
qaseeda (pl. qasaid)	ode
qibla	direction of prayer (i.e., facing Mecca)
qubba (pl. qubbab)	domed tomb of holy man
raka'a (pl. rukkat)	night prayer
rida	capital offense of apostasy
rukuba	lean-to porch
rukun (pl. arkaan)	lit., "corner," metaphor for public debate
sahur	pre-dawn Ramadan meal
salaam	peace
salat-a-subuh	morning prayer
salat-a-jenaza	funeral prayer over the deceased
saloon	from "salon," a parlor
samadi	total fast from eating and drinking
shahada	"witness," the basic Islamic belief
sharia	Islamic law
sheikh	head of a Sufi group, lit., "chief"
shirik	idolatry

sibha	carved prayer beads
silsila	the chain of religious history or knowledge
simaya	infant naming ceremony
sirwaal	baggy pants
subuh	predawn prayer
sunna	personal practice (of the Prophet)
talmith	pupil (apprentice)
tawhid	monotheism, unity
tajweed	recitation
tariqa	Sufi sect (lit., approach, method)
taub-a-sudani	Sudanese woman's outer covering garment
tummy	Gezira cracking clay
ulema	traditionally minded religious scholars
ummah	the Muslim community confronting the modern world
um rigayga	okra stew
Ustadh	teacher
wadu	ablutions
wafd	delegation
wali (pl. awlia)	holy man (deceased)
warid	divinely inspired insight
zahir	revealed
zar	a folk cult of charms and magic that had pre-Islamic origins
zei islami	"Islamic dress"
zowiya	place of Sufi lodging

GLOSSARY OF SUDANESE ARABIC TERMS

For Further Reading

An-Na'im, Abdullahi Ahmed. *Toward an Islamic Reformation: Civil Liberties, Human Rights and International Law.* Syracuse, NY: Syracuse University Press, 1990.

Armstrong, Karen. *Islam: A Short History.* New York: Modern Library, 2000.

Chittick, William C. *Sufism, A Short Introduction.* Oxford: One World Publications, 2000.

Daly, M. W., ed. *Al Majdhubiyya and Al Mikashifiyya: Two Sufi Tariqas in the Sudan.* Khartoum: Graduate College Publications, University of Khartoum, 1985.

Howard, W. Stephen. "Mahmoud Mohamed Taha: A Remarkable Teacher in Sudan." *Northeast African Studies* 10, no. 1 (1988): 83–93.

Karrar, Ali Salih. *The Sufi Brotherhoods in the Sudan.* Evanston, IL: Northwestern University Press, 1992.

Mahmoud, Mohamed A. *Quest for Divinity: A Critical Examination of the Thought of Mahmud Muhammad Taha.* Syracuse, NY: Syracuse University Press, 2007.

Safi, Omar, ed. *Progressive Muslims: On Justice, Gender and Pluralism.* Oxford: One World Publications, 2003.

Taha, Mahmoud Mohamed. *The Second Message of Islam.* Translated by Abdullahi Ahmed An-Na'im. Syracuse, NY: Syracuse University Press, 1987.

Thomas, Edward. *Islam's Perfect Stranger: The Life of Mahmud Muhammad Taha, Muslim Reformer of Sudan.* London: I. B. Tauris, 2010.